Excavation of Prehistoric and Romano-British Sites
at Marnel Park and Merton Rise (Popley) Basingstoke, 2004–8

By
James Wright, Andrew B. Powell and Alistair Barclay

Excavation of Prehistoric and Romano-British Sites
at Marnel Park and Merton Rise (Popley) Basingstoke, 2004–8

By
James Wright, Andrew B. Powell and Alistair Barclay

with contributions by
Catherine Barnett, Philippa Bradley, Nicholas Cooke, Dave Godden, Jessica M. Grimm, Kevin Hayward, Matt Leivers, Jacqueline I. McKinley, David Norcott, Ruth Pelling, Rachael Seager Smith, Chris J. Stevens and Sarah F. Wyles

and illustrations by
Karen Nichols and S.E. James

Wessex Archaeology 2009

Published 2009 by Wessex Archaeology Ltd
Portway House, Old Sarum Park, Salisbury, SP4 6EB
http://www.wessexarch.co.uk/

Copyright © 2009 Wessex Archaeology Ltd
All rights reserved

British Library Cataloguing in Publication Data
A catalogue record for this book is available from the British Library

ISBN 978-1-874350-51-4

Produced by Karen Nichols
Cover design by Karen Nichols

Printed by Cromwell Press Group, Trowbridge

Front cover: Late Iron Age/Romano-British settlement at Area A South, Merton Rise

Back cover: Excavation of a Romano-British corn drier at Area D North, Marnel Park

Wessex Archaeology Ltd is a registered charity No. 287786

Contents

List of Figures vi
Acknowledgements vii
Abstract viii
Preface, *by Paul Chadwick*. ix

Introduction
Geology, soils, and topography 1
Archaeological background 2

Results
Early Neolithic to Early Bronze Age 3
    Discussion 6
Middle to Late Bronze Age 7
    Burnt flint features 11
    Discussion 11
Early Iron Age 13
    Area A South 13
    Area A East 14
    Area F 16
    Landscape division 17
    Discussion 19
Late Iron Age/Romano-British 19
    Area A South and North 20
        Area A South 20
        Area A North 24
    Area D South and North 26
        Area D South 26
        Area D North 29
    Area C 34
    Discussion 35

Bibliography 37

Specialist Reports

Part 1: Finds
Human bone, *by Jacqueline I. McKinley*
Coins, *by Nicholas Cooke*
Metalwork, *by Rachael Seager Smith*
Worked flint, *by Philippa Bradley and Matt Leivers*
Prehistoric pottery, *by Alistair Barclay*
Late Iron Age and Romano-British pottery,
    by Rachael Seager Smith
Worked stone, *by Kevin Hayward*
Coral bead, *by Alistair Barclay*
Miscellaneous finds, *by Rachael Seager Smith*

Part 2: Environmental Remains
Animal bone, *by Jessica M. Grimm*
Molluscs, *by Sarah F. Wyles*
Charred plant remains, *by Ruth Pelling*
Charcoal, *by Catherine Barnett*
Radiocarbon dating, *by Alistair Barclay*
    and Chris J. Stevens

These reports are available online at:

http://www.wessexarch.co.uk/projects/hampshire/popley

List of Figures

Figure 1. General location x
Figure 2. Other sites mentioned in the text 1
Figure 3. Distribution of prehistoric features and findspots 3
Figure 4. Neolithic-Early Bronze Age pits 5
Figure 5. Area C2 showing area of possible 'barrow'. 6
Figure 6. Prehistoric features in Areas A East and F4 7
Figure 7. Middle Bronze Age pottery. 8
Figure 8. Middle Bronze Age pit D50203: section 8
Figure 9. Comparative plans of post-built roundhouses and six-post structure 10
Figure 10. Early Iron Age pottery 12
Figure 11. Prehistoric features in Area A South 13
Figure 12. Detailed plan of roundhouses A50029 and A50100 15
Figure 13. Coral bead 17
Figure 14. Areas B and F: Wessex Linear ditches and plan of Area B2 showing hearth 18
Figure 15. Distribution of Late Iron Age/Romano-British features 20
Figure 16. Late Iron Age/Romano-British features in Area A South 21
Figure 17. Late Iron Age/Romano-British pottery from Area A South 22
Figure 18. Sections of wells in Area A South and chalk spindlewhorl 23
Figure 19. Late Iron Age/Romano-British features in Area A North. 25
Figure 20. Area D: all phases 26
Figure 21. Area D South: all phases 27
Figure 22. Area D North: all phases 29
Figure 23. Area D North: cremation graves with selected finds 30
Figure 24. Corn drier in Area D North: section 31
Figure 25. Late Iron Age/Romano-British pottery from Area D 32
Figure 26. Copper alloy objects 33
Figure 27. Romano-British features in Area C, with section of quarry C8104 34

Acknowledgements

The project was commissioned by CgMs Consulting Ltd on behalf of David Wilson Homes and Hampshire County Council (Property, Business and Regulatory Services). Wessex Archaeology would like to thank Ray Goodenough of David Wilson Homes, Peter Reed of Hope and Clay, Nigel Hull of Blaze Construction, Rebecca Thompson, Chris Peake, and Louise Hague of Hampshire County Council, and Paul Chadwick of CgMs Consulting for their help and assistance during the course of the project. Kevin Stubbs of Bursledon Brickworks Museum provided useful information about corn driers and is gratefully acknowledged. Thanks are also due to Stephen Appleby and David Hopkins of Hampshire County Council's Environment Department who monitored the project on behalf of the Local Planning Authority.

The various stages of fieldwork were led by James Wright, Dave Godden, Jon Martin, and Ruth Panes with the assistance of Nick Best, Bob Davis, Mike Dinwiddy, and Dave Norcott. Ruth Pelling wishes to thank Gill Campbell for providing her unpublished report on the plant remains from Grateley, Hampshire.

The project was managed in the field by Nick Truckle and during post-excavation by Alistair Barclay, assisted by Andrew Powell. Julie Gardiner, Karen Walker, David Hopkins and Paul Chadwick read and provided useful comments on the text. The report was typeset for publication by Karen Nichols.

The archive will be deposited with the Hampshire County Museum Service (reference WA 58570–8, 59320–5).

Abstract

This report brings together the archaeological results from two fieldwork investigations at Popley, Basingstoke (NGR 463 154), now known as Merton Rise and Marnel Park, in advance of housing development. The archaeological work took place during 2004–8.

The two projects provided a good opportunity to investigate 59 ha of mostly chalk downland that was known from the preliminary investigations to contain prehistoric, Romano-British, and later remains. A landscape approach, achieved through targeted interventions, allowed for a greater understanding of the immediate environs of the identified settlements. The project revealed ephemeral traces of human activity during the Neolithic and Early Bronze Age, characterised by sparse finds of flintwork and pottery and occasional pit deposits containing the refuse from domestic occupation which included Grooved Ware and Beaker pottery. One of the Beaker pits produced early evidence for cereal cultivation on the site.

The first tangible evidence for permanent settlement occurred from about 1500 BC onwards with the discovery of a series of open settlements characterised by post-built roundhouses and associated with Deverel-Rimbury pottery. The remains of some 15 buildings, mostly roundhouses, were investigated that varied in date from Middle Bronze Age to Early Iron Age and typically showed a change in design from a small basic form to larger and more elaborate architecture. Radiocarbon dates were obtained for two of these structures. Charred plant remains indicate that the inhabitants of these settlements were involved in cereal cultivation. Evidence for other activities in the landscape included an extensive burnt flint spread and a small number of features of related character, one of which was radiocarbon dated to the Late Bronze Age. Their precise function is unknown, although they may have involved the heating of water or generation of steam for industrial, domestic, or other social/ritual purposes. Major landscape division is also a feature at this time, and appears to have occurred sometime after the first roundhouse was constructed and perhaps towards the end of the Late Bronze Age when there is evidence from the immediate area for settlement intensification and expansion.

Little evidence for Middle Iron Age activity was recovered, although it is possible that settlement shifted to adjacent areas during this phase such as a possible banjo enclosure that is suggested from cropmarks at Merton Rise. The Late Iron Age was another period of significant change that witnessed the creation of new settlements, enclosures, and trackways, while there is also evidence for the re-use of older boundary ditches. Field lynchets and the evidence for field clearance indicate that some of the land that had previously been used for pasture was now being used for arable. There was a notable contrast between the relatively short-lived and specialised enclosures, probably for animal husbandry, that were excavated at Merton Rise on the chalk compared with the long-lived complex of enclosures that occurred on poorer draining soils at Marnel Park. These poorer soils may also explain the apparent low status of this settlement, which exhibited only partly Romanised and mostly rural characteristics. After the abandonment of the settlement in the 4th century the land appears to have been used mostly for agricultural purposes.

Preface

Since its introduction in 1990, the government's policy guidance on archaeology (*Planning Policy Guidance 16 Archaeology and Planning*) has attracted criticism from a variety of sources; landowners and developers have frequently commented on the cost of archaeological investigations, particularly when the end product is a confusing jumble of post-holes, a fistful of battered pottery sherds, and a dry report published in an obscure technical journal. Equally, university archaeologists have bemoaned the unstructured investigation of random and often unrelated parts of the landscape which have nothing in common other than being the subject of development proposals. Additional frustration is added by the policy which preserves the most important archaeological sites, leaving today's archaeologists to investigate only second division sites!

Fortuitously, the allocation of adjacent plots of land totalling 59 ha for development in the Basingstoke and Deane Local Plan created an opportunity to address these criticisms head on. The investigation of one of the largest tracts of chalk landscape with an adjacent area of Reading Beds provided an unparalleled opportunity to unravel the long and complex settlement and farming history on a scale rarely attempted.

Between 2004 and 2008 a phased strategy was adopted on behalf of both the public sector landowner, Hampshire County Council, and a private sector house builder, David Wilson Homes, which, via the use of geophysical survey and trial trenching, identified and narrowed-down areas of particular archaeological interest, enabling resources to be targeted on excavation and recording of the key locations in the landscape where settlement activity was concentrated.

The resulting report, which I hope strikes a reasonable balance between the essential task of archaeological reporting and 'telling the story of this place' will not be buried unread on remote library shelves, but is to be given to local interest groups, local schools, and others with an interest in heritage and the evolution of the landscape of Hampshire and the hinterland of Silchester Roman town.

The results speak for themselves, but whereas in 2004 our understanding of the archaeology north of Basingstoke was based on a handful of prehistoric flints and air photographs of an undated but suspected prehistoric enclosure, we now have a detailed understanding of 3000 years of land division, prehistoric and Roman settlement, and farming.

The excavations have yielded no particularly spectacular discoveries; no gold coins, no rich burials, and no mosaic pavements, but the everyday houses, barns, cattle corrals, and fields of ordinary prehistoric and Roman farming folk have been revealed providing a hitherto unsuspected time depth to North Popley and Basingstoke.

Paul Chadwick
CgMs Consulting

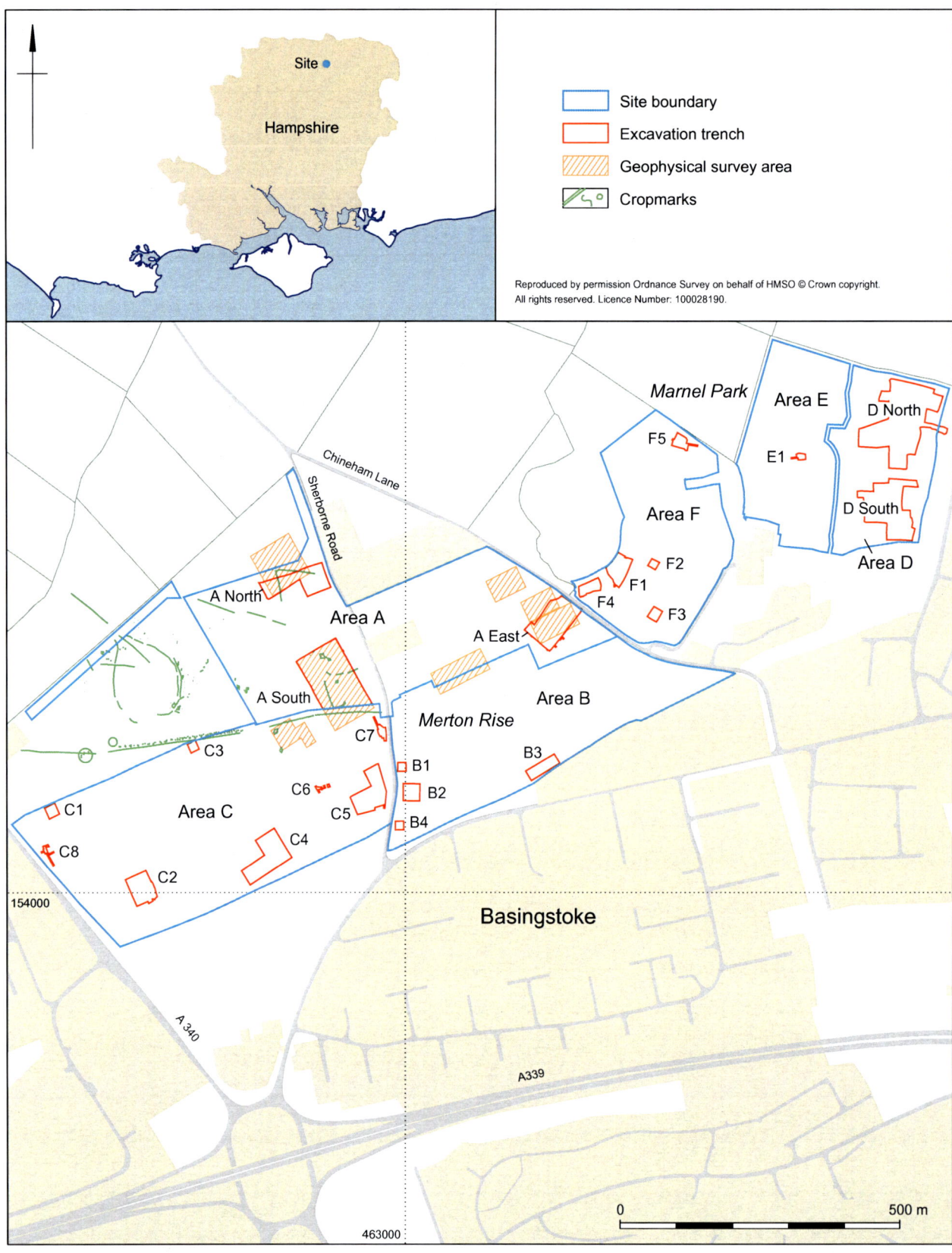

Figure 1 General location

Introduction

A programme of archaeological fieldwork undertaken between December 2004 and June 2008, in advance of two housing developments on the north side of Basingstoke, provided an opportunity to examine the development of a prehistoric and rural Romano-British landscape covering 59 ha of chalkland (NGR 463 154). The works, commissioned by CgMs Consulting and generously funded by David Wilson Homes and Hampshire County Council, fell within two main blocks of land, respectively – at Merton Rise, extending from the A340 Aldermaston Road at the west to Chineham Lane at the east, and at Marnel Park (originally called Popley Fields) between Chineham Lane and Carpenter's Down (Fig. 1).

Preliminary stages of work included desk-based assessments (CgMs 1997; 2002), geophysical survey (GSB Prospection 2002), aerial photographic plotting, and fieldwalking, as well as a watching brief at Marnel Park during the creation of a newt corridor (Foundations Archaeology 2005). During evaluation stages, arrays of trial trenches representing an approximate 3.5% sample of the development areas were machine-excavated across both sites, comprising 285 trenches (plus a further 20 smaller trenches and trench extensions) at Merton Rise, and 111 trenches at Marnel Park. The results of the evaluations informed the excavation strategy, determining the locations and extents of the excavation trenches.

In both areas the fieldwork was undertaken in stages before the various phases of development began, each site being subdivided by the developers into separate areas - Areas A–C at Merton Rise and Phases 1–3 at Marnel Park (Fig. 1). At Merton Rise three excavation trenches were opened in Area A, referred to below as A East, North and South. Three small trenches and an area of test-pits were excavated at Area B (B1–B4), and small trenches at Area C (C1–C8). For the sake of consistency, the three fieldwork areas at Marnel Park are referred to below as Areas D–F, with two trenches in Area D (D North and South) and in Area F (F1–F5). As Merton Rise and Marnel Park were two separate excavation projects, all context numbers in this report have been given their Area letter prefix to prevent repetition.

Geology, Soils, and Topography

Areas A–C, and the south-western part of Area F, lie on the Upper Chalk, which was overlain by a topsoil of greyish-brown silty clay loam (Fig. 2). The north-eastern part of Area F, and Areas D and E, however, fall within a *c.* 500 m wide band of Reading Beds which overlies the Chalk, comprising clays, silt, and fine grained sand. The contrasting geology and soils was particularly evident in the poorer visibility of features cutting the predominantly clay soils of the Reading Beds, and the stratigraphic relationship between them. To the north, the Reading Beds are overlain by London Clay (Geological Survey of Great Britain, Sheet 284, 1981).

The rolling downland on which the site lies is bisected to the south by the east- and then north-flowing River Loddon, a tributary of the Thames, and

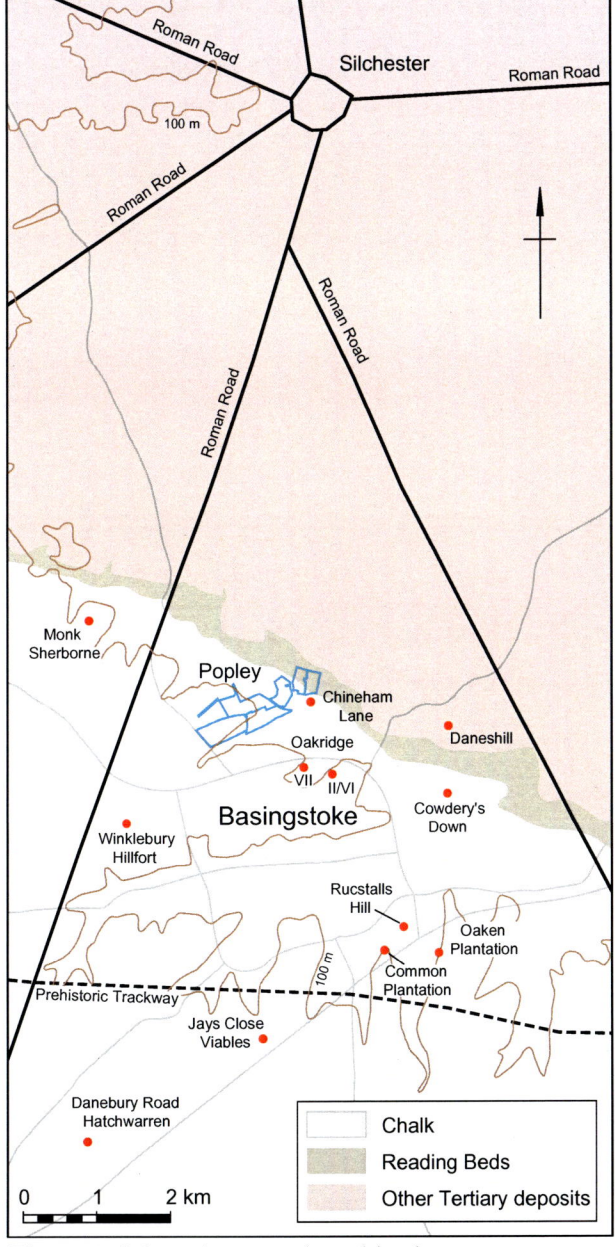

Figure 2 Other sites mentioned in the text

more locally by north-east aligned dry valleys. Areas A–C, at *c.* 85–116 m above Ordnance Datum (aOD), lie on the north side of one such dry valley, with Area F on the south and north facing slopes and plateau of a ridge that descends to the east (Fig. 2.1). Area D, at 81–8 m aOD, lies on a gentle north-east facing slope south of a steeper, south-west facing slope, with an east-flowing stream at the north of the site discharging into the River Loddon 4 km to the east.

Archaeological Background

The evidence for later prehistoric settlement and funerary activity within the immediate area is well-documented, with a Middle Bronze Age cremation cemetery recorded at Daneshill (Millett and Schadla-Hall 1991), and Late Bronze Age/Early Iron Age pits and post-holes at Chineham Lane (Boismier *et al.* 1998; Fig. 2). The Iron Age hillfort at Winklebury, excavated by Smith (1977), is only 2 km to the south-west of the site and the well-known Iron Age settlement at Cowdery's Down is only 2 km to the south-east (Millett with James 1983). Other Iron Age settlements have been recorded at Brighton Hill South (Coe and Newman 1992; Fasham *et al.* 1995; Howell and Durden 2005) and Rooksdown Hospital (Butterworth 1994).

Marnel Park lies only 6 km south of the Roman *civitas* capital of *Calleva* (Silchester) and is between two converging Roman roads that connect *Calleva* to *Venta* and *Noviomagus* (Winchester and Chichester). The expansion of Basingstoke over the last 30 years has lead to the discovery and recording of several Romano-British settlements – at Rucstalls Hill (Oliver and Applin 1978), Daneshill (Millett and Schadla Hall 1991), Oakridge (Oliver 1992), Brighton Hill South (Coe and Newman 1992; Howell and Durden 2005), and Jays Close (Viables Two) (Millett and Russell 1984; Gibson 2004).

Results

Early Neolithic to Early Bronze Age

The earliest evidence indicates that the area was at least visited during the Early and Middle Neolithic, and possibly during the Mesolithic, although the limited evidence did not establish the nature of the activities undertaken. A number of pieces of possible Mesolithic flintwork were recovered, including two scrapers from Area A and some blades from Areas A, C, and D, but none is particularly distinctive and could equally be of Early Neolithic date. Flints of more certain Early Neolithic date were recovered from a solution hollow in Area F and as redeposited material across much of the site. In addition, two residual sherds of Early Neolithic pottery were recovered from later features in Areas A and F. Similarly, the only evidence of Middle Neolithic activity was two small abraded body sherds of Peterborough Ware recovered from a tree-throw hole in Area F4; the flint-tempered sherds, probably from the same vessel, are decorated with twisted cord impressions, that on the larger sherd appearing to form part of a herringbone motif.

The site produced slightly more substantial evidence for Late Neolithic and Early Bronze Age activity, largely in the form of a small number of pits containing deposits of settlement refuse, possibly token in character (see Garrow 2007, 12), including first Grooved Ware, then Beaker, pottery. This activity was concentrated in Area A (Fig. 3), although residual Beaker pottery was recovered from other parts of the site.

A number of features in Area A East produced a small assemblage of plain and decorated Grooved Ware pottery and flintwork. Of particular note was pit A50384, measuring 0.9 m diameter (Fig. 4), whose lower fill produced 14 Grooved Ware sherds (160 g) (Fig. 4, 1–3), 82 pieces of worked flint, and other domestic debris, including burnt flint, animal bone (mostly cattle, but also pig), and fragments of fired clay, as well as many fragments of charred hazelnut shell and charcoal (mostly alder, but also oak, hazel, and pomaceaous fruit wood). The pottery, comprising decorated body and/or base sherds, came from approximately six different vessels, both thin- and thick-walled, in a range of fabrics containing inclusions of grog and shell/sand. The decoration

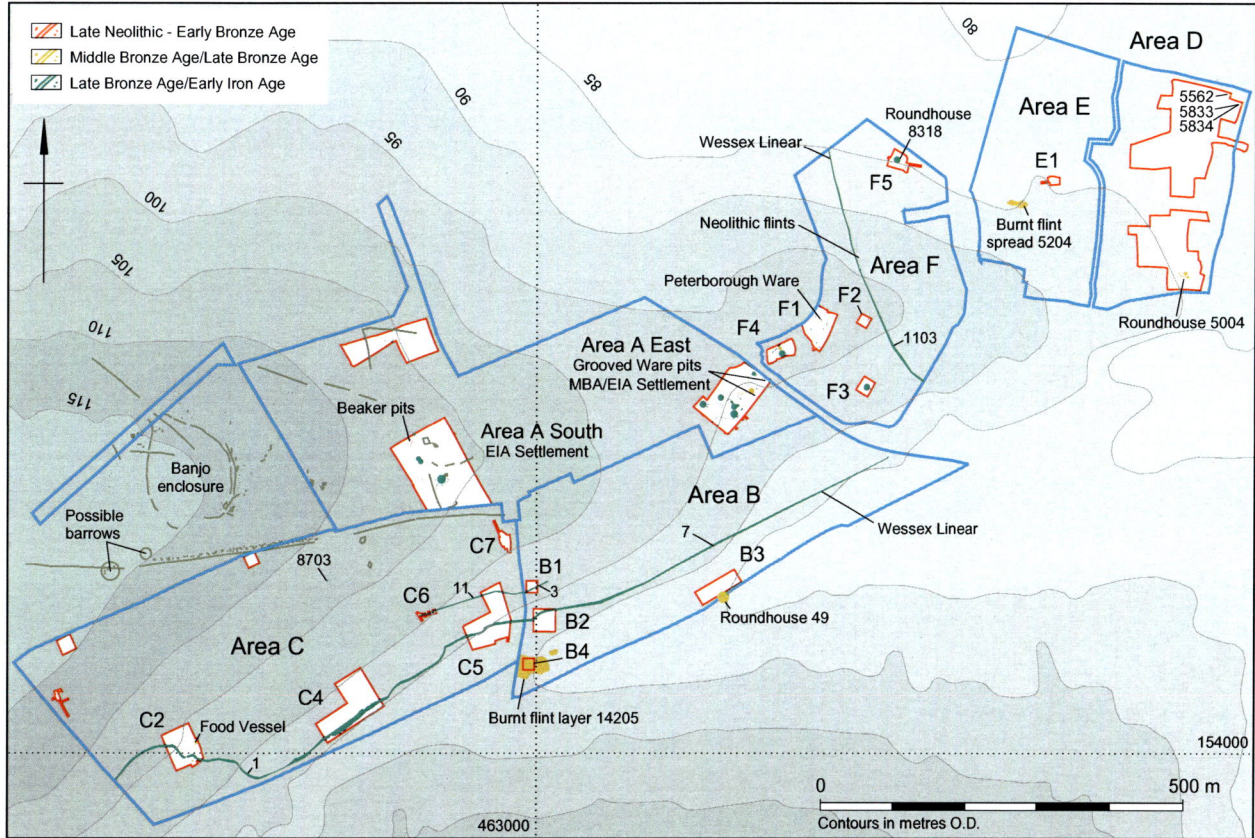

Figure 3 Distribution of prehistoric features and findspots

consists of relatively wide shallow grooves, incised lines, fingernail impressions, and deeper shorter grooved lines, with infilled panels and all-over herringbone. An incised decorated vessel appears to show infilled vertical panels separated by one or more pairs of incised lines. No complete profiles are represented, although one base may derive from a jar, while a second base, at a shallower angle, is from a bowl. Overall, the forms and decoration can be accommodated within the Durrington Walls substyle (Longworth 1971, figs 47–8). There is relatively little Grooved Ware from this area of Hampshire or indeed from the adjacent areas of Wiltshire, Berkshire, and Surrey (Longworth and Cleal 1999; Barclay 1999; Cotton 2004, 26). To the north of the Basingstoke area, in the Upper Kennet valley, it is virtually absent, and when it does occur it tends to be found in small quantities (Barclay 2004, 57–8; Cleal 1991–3, 19).

The worked flints from this pit are typical of assemblages associated with Grooved Ware. They are dominated by flakes (76), many of which are cortical, the flint having been fairly carefully worked with platform edge preparation noted on many. A few almost blade-like removals were noted amongst the flakes, some of which have use-wear. The two cores both have two platforms at right-angles to each other (Fig. 4, 4). The three scrapers have been quite neatly worked, one having been made on a side trimming flake (Fig. 4, 5). A miscellaneous retouched piece may have been from a knife (Fig. 4, 6). No small chips were recovered indicating that this was not *in situ* knapping debris but the collected residue of domestic activity. Both used and burnt pieces were noted, as well as flakes in very fresh condition, a feature that has been noted elsewhere (Bradley 1999, 214–17).

The single fill of a similar-sized oval pit (A50387) (Fig. 4), 27 m to the north-east of pit A50384, contained a further five sherds of plain Grooved Ware and some burnt flint (as well as one of the Early Neolithic sherds, above), while a further small sherd of Grooved Ware or Beaker was recovered from pit A50382, 22m to the west.

Flints comparable with those from pit A50384 (along with a single sherd of Neolithic/Bronze Age pottery) were also recovered from an area of intercutting Early Iron Age pits (A50197) toward the centre of Area A East (Fig. 6). Among the few retouched forms were a scraper and a knife, both consistent with a Late Neolithic date. A keeled core was also recovered, a type that is frequently associated with Late Neolithic assemblages (Healy 1985). The flints had suffered limited post-depositional damage, and appear to have derived from one or more Late Neolithic features that had been truncated by the digging of the later pits. Other flints of probable Neolithic or Early Bronze Age date, including scrapers, serrated flakes, and piercers, were recovered from across the wider site.

Activity, similar in character and possibly similar in function, continued in the same general area during the Early Bronze Age, with three adjacent circular pits (A55227, A55243, and A55245), containing Beaker/Early Bronze Age pottery, arranged in a shallow arc in Area A South (Fig. 11). The pits were 0.8–1.1 m in diameters and up to 0.3 m deep (Fig. 4). In the northern pit (A55227) the upper fill contained two Beaker sherds (Fig. 4, 7–8), worked and burnt flint, fragments of animal bone (pig humerus), burnt hazelnut shells, three indeterminate cereal grains, and charcoal (elm and blackthorn/cherry). One of the sherds is from a rusticated vessel decorated with rows of plastic fingernail impressions; the other is from the neck of a Southern-style long-necked Beaker (see Clarke 1970), and has an incised geometric pattern, probably floating lozenges. The rusticated sherd could be from a similar style of vessel.

The lower fill in the adjacent pit (A55243) contained four Beaker sherds (Fig. 4, 9), along with worked flint, including three scrapers (Fig. 4, 10), fragments of animal bone (including a sheep/goat tibia), and hazelnut shells. The sherds are possibly from an all-over aplastic, fingernail impressed vessel, three possibly from a slight globular belly, the fourth possibly from the waist with the suggestion of a straight neck. Although the actual profile can not be precisely ascertained, there is the hint that it equates to the long necked or Southern styles (see Clarke 1970, 294, fig. 121).

The southern pit (A55245) had a dark lower fill containing an antler placed against the edge of the base, three sherds of pottery, 50 pieces of worked flint, fragments of burnt flint, animal bone (cattle humerus), charcoal (mostly elm), and hazelnut shells. One sherd was of Early Bronze Age pottery, but the other two plain sherds are of uncertain date and at least one would be difficult to accommodate within the Beaker style. The smaller sherd, which is relatively thin-walled (6 mm) with highly burnished reddish-brown surfaces and a black core, has the well-made appearance and 'sealing-wax' colour found in some Beakers, particularly of the Wessex Middle Rhine group (Clarke 1970). Plain Beaker vessels occur but are generally rare and may be early within the overall sequence (see Needham 2005). The other thin-walled sherd (5 mm), which had all-over aplastic fingernail impressions in an oxidised grog-tempered fabric, has close affinities with Beaker pottery and is similar in appearance to sherds from pit A55243.

Beaker pottery has a long currency from 2400 to 1700 cal BC (see Needham 2005). The sherds with aplastic fingernail impressions could be early within

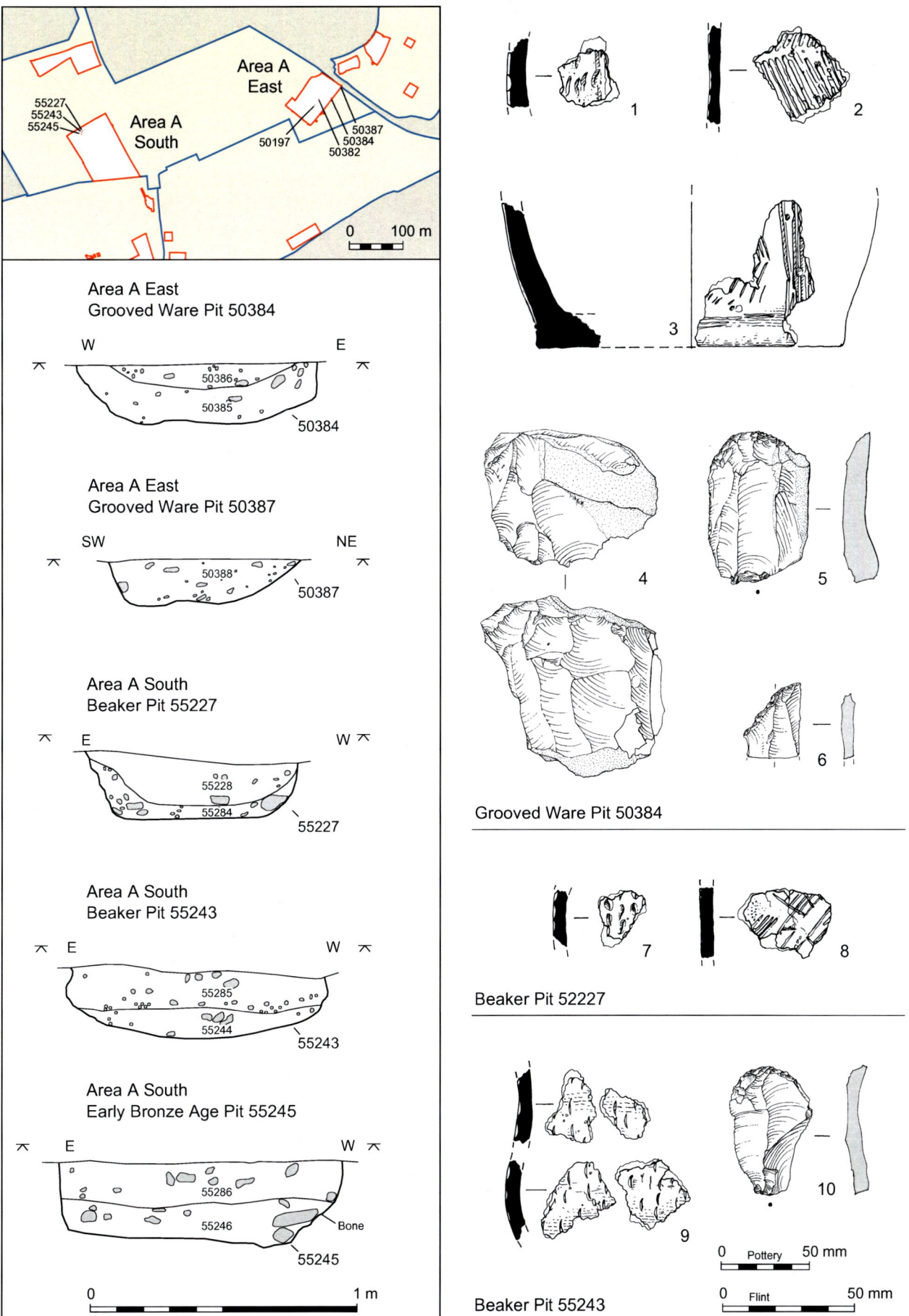

Figure 4 Neolithic–Early Bronze Age pits: sections with selected finds

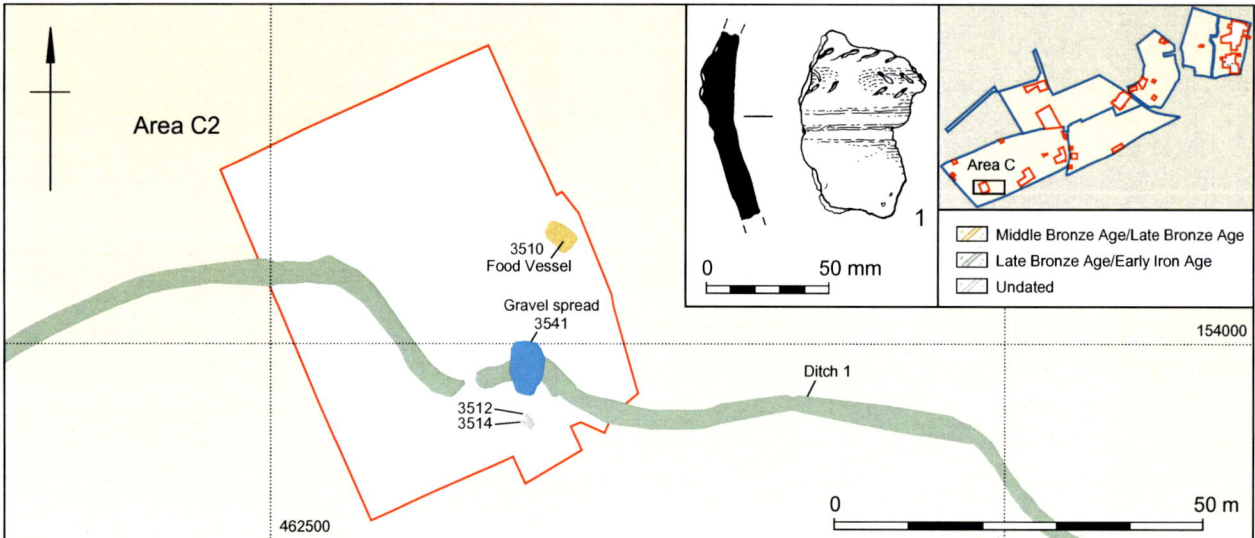

Figure 5 Area C2 showing area of possible 'barrow'

this sequence, as vessels with this type of decoration are known to occur throughout the later 3rd millennium cal BC (eg, Bury St Edmunds, Suffolk and Chilbolton, Hampshire (3780±80 BP; 2340–1940 cal BC; OxA-1073); Needham 2005, figs 5.10 and 10.2). In contrast, the sherd with floating lozenge motif and the one with plastic fingernail impressed decoration are possibly later in date and on typological grounds are more likely to belong to the early 2nd millennium cal BC (see Needham 2005).

In Area C2, a large shoulder sherd (30 g) from a decorated Food Vessel (Fig. 5, 1) was recovered from the fill of tree-throw hole C3510. It can be accommodated within the Southern Bipartite Vase group (Burgess 1980, 87), although its stopped shoulder groove is a feature of the so-called Yorkshire Vase style (Burgess 1980, 87, and fig. 3.1, 5–6). It appears to have been overfired/refired, which could indicate that it has come into contact with a cremation pyre (see Barclay 2002). Food Vessels are generally found throughout Britain, although they are less common in southern England.

Approximately 20 m south of where the Food Vessel sherd was found, there were two adjacent 'grave-shaped' features (C3512 and C3514) located within a marked bend of the later Wessex Linear ditch (below; Fig. 5). One possible reason for the line of the ditch is that it was routed so to avoid an existing feature in the landscape, perhaps a mound covering these two 'graves', although the absence from either of any human bone (or other finds) means that such an interpretation is very tenuous. Nonetheless, it is possible that an oval spread of gravel (C3541) laid down to provide a compact surface at the point where a Romano-British trackway (C3, below) crossed the ditch (and the 'graves'; Fig. 27) could have derived from the levelling of such a mound.

Discussion

A local collector, G.W. Willis, amassed a huge quantity of flintwork collected from fields around the southern side of Basingstoke over many years of the first half of the 20th century. Analysis of his collection (Gardiner 1988, 414–23, fig. 9.6) indicated the presence of more than 50 predominantly Late Neolithic–Early Bronze Age surface flint scatters within a 12 km radius of the town, occurring at an average distance apart of about 1 km. The contents of these assemblages suggest locally intensive settlement activity. Willis was less active in the immediate area of Popley but recorded two scatters within 2.5 km to the west at Lone Barn and Shothanger's Farm (Gardiner 1988, cat. nos 119 and 185) which, in addition to large quantities of scrapers, produced several polished and roughout flint axes, a variety of arrowheads, and a range of flake and core tools indicative of domestic occupation.

A small number of Neolithic–Early Bronze Age barrows and prehistoric burials have been investigated in the Basingstoke area (Millett with James 1983) and cropmark evidence also suggests a number of ring-ditches (Fig. 1). Environmental evidence from the features excavated indicates the presence in the landscape of mixed woodland and scrub (containing oak, elm, hazel, ash, pomaceaous fruit wood, and blackthorn/cherry type), while the presence of alder indicates the exploitation of a damp environment such as along the courses of local streams.

While no evidence of cereal production was recovered from the Late Neolithic pits, the presence of cereal grains from one of the Beaker pits suggests that some level of cultivation, and hence possibly short-term, small-scale, and probably semi-sedentary settlement, had started by this period (Robinson 2000; Moffett, Robinson and Straker 1989). This picture may be reinforced by the presence of mature cattle and pig in the Late Neolithic and of sheep/goat in the Beaker period, although wild resources such as hazel appear to have continued to play a role in the subsistence economy. The lack of domestic or agricultural structures is not surprising given that few houses of this period are recorded nationally; most of the early features were on the plateau of the chalk ridge (Fig. 3) and any ephemeral traces of temporary shelters are likely to have been erased by recent agriculture.

Middle and Late Bronze Age

The first signs of permanent settlement of the area occur in the Middle Bronze Age (1600–1150 cal BC) with the construction of a small number of post-built roundhouses dispersed across the site (Fig. 3). The range of finds, including Deverel-Rimbury pottery, and environmental remains from the roundhouses and associated features suggest that they were probably domestic structures. Almost all the pottery is from relatively thick-walled Bucket Urns in a coarse flint-tempered fabric (Fig. 7, 1–4), with only a few thin-walled sherds in fine flint-tempered fabric from probable Globular Urns, and a single vessel, also possibly a Bucket Urn, containing grog in its fabric. There was also a general spread across the site of flintwork dating to this general period, characterised by roughly worked flakes and irregularly flaked cores, with retouched pieces, mainly scrapers and retouched flakes, being generally perfunctorily worked.

Much of the evidence for Middle Bronze Age settlement came from Area A East (Fig. 6). Part of one possible roundhouse, with a projected diameter of *c.* 6.2 m, was represented by an arc of five heavily truncated post-holes (A50199; Figs 6 and 9). One post-hole (A50361) contained a single Bucket Urn sherd; another (A50399) contained 30 sherds, probably from one or more Bucket Urns, while others produced worked and/or burnt flint. An irregular,

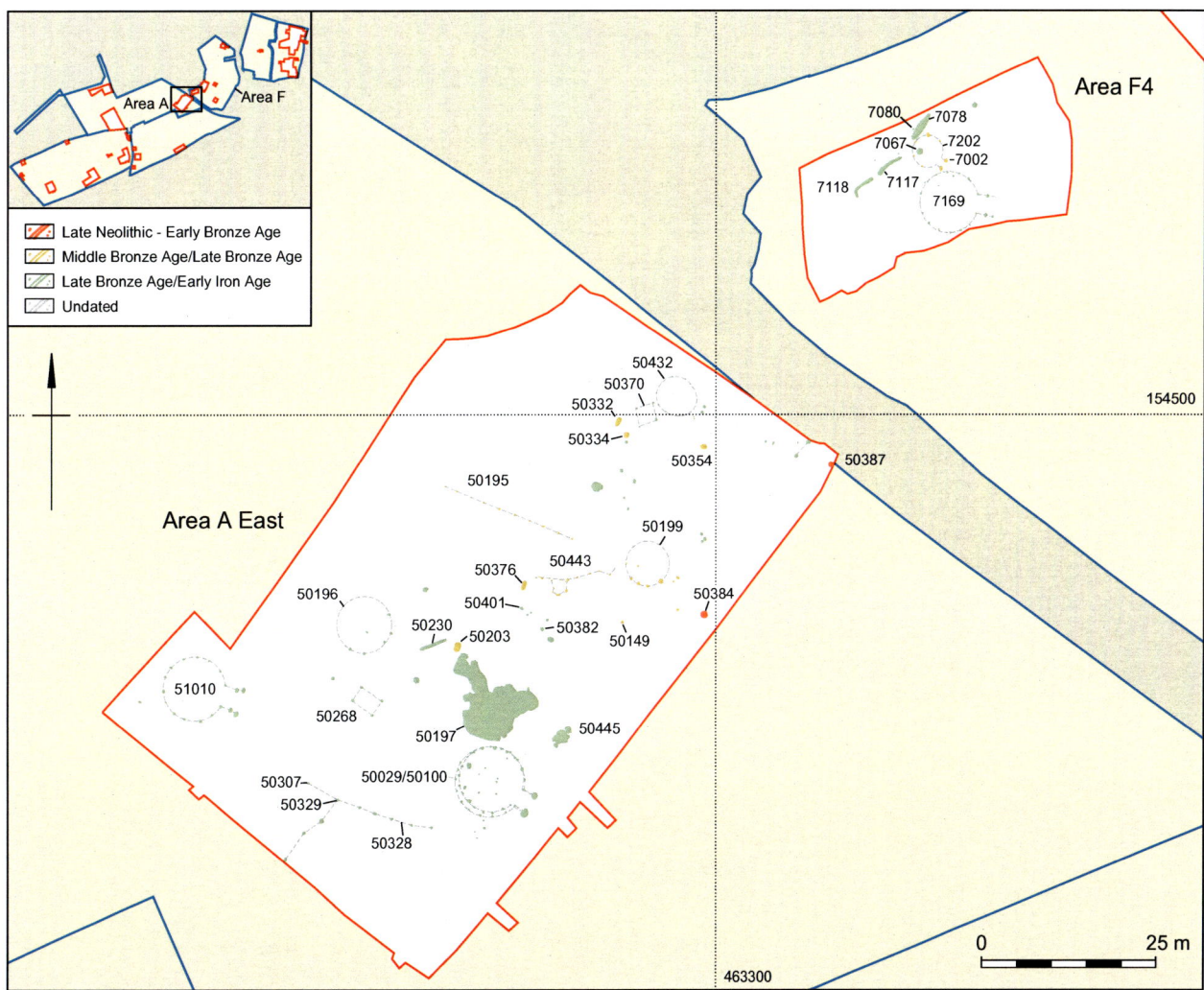

Figure 6 Prehistoric features in Areas A East and F4

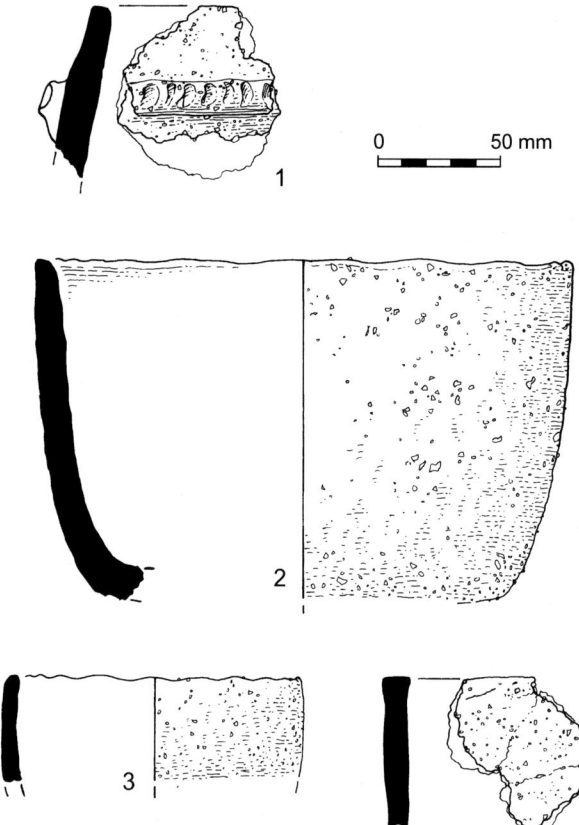

Figure 7 Middle Bronze Age pottery

10 m long line of 14 undated post-holes (A50443), of varying size, shape, and spacing, ran west from the structure, and may be associated with it (alternatively it may be associated with the Early Iron Age roundhouses and fence-lines in the same area, see below).

There were a number of pits in the same general area (A50149, A50203, A50376, A50332, A50334, and A50354; Fig. 6), as well as pit F7509 in Area F1 to the east, many of them oval in shape (averaging c. 0.8 x 1.2 m) but varying in depth (0.1–0.9 m), containing varying quantities of domestic refuse including pottery, worked and burnt flint, and animal bone. The smallest pit (A50149), which was 0.4 m in diameter and 0.13 m deep, contained over 50 sherds (1085 g), possibly from a single Bucket Urn placed on its base, while a larger, and the deepest oval pit (A50203; Fig. 8) also contained a relatively large group of Bucket Urn sherds (66 sherds, 1314 g) and animal bone (skull fragments and vertebrae of cattle and sheep/goat, mostly from adult animals). Pit A50332, measuring 0.7 x 1.3 m and 0.1 m deep, was filled largely with unworked flint nodules. These pits also contained varying quantities of charred plant remains and charcoal, the lower fill of one 0.4 m deep oval pit (A50354) containing charred grains of spelt/emmer and charcoal fragments, along with a rim sherd from a Bucket Urn with a cordoned shoulder with fingertip printing (Fig. 7, 1). A number of abraded sherds recovered from the area of intercutting Late Bronze Age pits (below) in the centre of Area A East, could belong to either Deverel-Rimbury or post-Deverel-Rimbury vessels, perhaps indicating that the later activity had disturbed further features of Middle Bronze Age date.

Similar evidence was found to the west, on the southern edge of Area B3, where a group of features was recorded in the base of a dry valley, sealed by up to 0.7 m of colluvium (below). They included an arc of five post-holes, spaced 1.1–2.3 m apart, and two internal post-holes, probably representing part another roundhouse (B49), which at c. 10.5 m in diameter would have been significantly larger than the other structures of this period (Fig. 9). Two of the post-holes (B16 and B15103) contained sherds of Middle Bronze Age date, B16 also containing a deposit of typical arable weed seeds suggesting cereal processing within the structure. Further finds of probable domestic refuse were recovered from two probably associated pits, one (B21) lying within the arc, the other (B15) just outside, and a tree-throw hole (also within the arc). Pit B15, for example, which was at least 1.1 m wide and 0.3 m deep, produced over 1 kg of Deverel-Rimbury pottery from its lowest fill (Fig. 7, 2), along with unidentifiable fragments of animal bone, charcoal, and charred cereal grains, possibly representing a dump of hearth material; the overlying fill produced fewer finds.

Structural evidence was also found to the east, in Area D South, where an arc of five post-holes, and

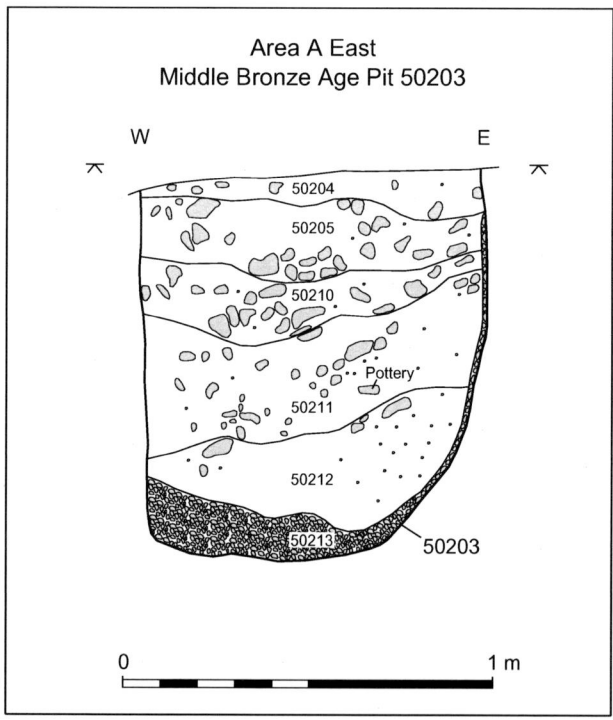

Figure 8 Middle Bronze Age pit D50203: section

two slots flanking a south-east facing entrance, formed a small sub-circular structure (D5004), measuring *c.* 4.6 m front to back by 5.4 m wide, with a large central post-hole (Figs 9 and 21). The fills of the post-holes and slots consisted almost entirely of burnt flint with small quantities of charcoal, the only find being a small sherd in coarse flint-tempered fabric, possibly from an ovoid jar. Further fragmentary sherds – from a thick-walled coarseware jar and a small ovoid-shaped vessel (Fig. 7, 3), and a finger-tip impressed sherd from a relatively thin-walled vessel – were recovered from a large pit or waterhole (D5001) located immediately in front of the roundhouse entrance. The position of the pit, excavated to a depth of 1.3 m, suggests it may not have been exactly contemporary with the roundhouse, and since most of the finds from it, including a saddle quern, a cylindrical loomweight, and an antler pick, came from its uppermost fill, there is little indication as to when the feature was dug. The loomweight was of a type that is fairly common on Middle-Late Bronze Age sites, and was probably used in an upright, warp-weighted wooden framed loom (Burgess 1980, 278).

The dating of the small pottery assemblage from the Area D features is uncertain due to the lack of diagnostic sherds, the small ovoid jars, having affinities with either Middle Bronze Age Deverel-Rimbury assemblages or Plain Ware assemblages of the Late Bronze Age. An insubstantial gully (D5290), 0.2 m wide and 0.1 m deep, that curved around the south-western side of the structure may be associated; it contained three sherds of Late Bronze Age pottery, as well as a piece of worked flint and some burnt flint.

Possibly also of this date, although the dating evidence is ambiguous, was small roundhouse (F7202) in Area F4 (Figs 6 and 9). It comprised an irregular circle, *c.* 5 m in diameter, of six post-holes, most set at 2 m intervals but with gaps at the south and east where further post-holes may have been truncated. A piece of charred sloe, possibly derived from an internal heath, recovered from a larger than average post-hole (F7082) probably flanking the entrance at the south-east, produced a calibrated radiocarbon date of 1610–1450 cal BC (KIA-37130: 3255±25 BP 95%), which falls within the earlier part of the Middle Bronze Age. The same post-hole also produced a worn sherd (2 g) from a plain ware jar of Late Bronze Age date (1150–850 BC). A large pit within the interior of the structure was of later date.

In addition to evidence for settlement activity, a range of features indicating non-domestic activity was also identified in this period. It is possible, for example, that two unurned cremation burials in Area D South, both undated, were broadly contemporary with structure D5004 (Fig. 21). Both were in small, shallow, circular graves, one (D5082), 10 m to the north-east, containing the remains of an adult, the other (D5095, 50 m to the north-west, containing the remains of an adult and neonate. A small quantity of cremated human bone was also recovered from a shallow oval pit (D2903) recorded just north-east of the area during the evaluation phase. Alternatively, these graves may be broadly contemporary with the Romano-British urned cremation burials (and one unurned but probably Romano-British burial) excavated in Area D North (below).

A feature (C8703), possibly a tree-throw hole, in Area C appears to represent specialised flint knapping activity at a distance from any domestic context (Fig. 3). It contained the vast majority (603 pieces) of the Middle–Late Bronze Age flint assemblage (as well as representing 32% of the total flint assemblage from the site). The group consists entirely of unretouched debitage - flakes, a single blade, cores, core fragments, chips, and pieces of irregular waste – but contains no retouched pieces. It also has an under-representation of primary flakes, suggesting that flint nodules were being partially worked and the debris dumped into the hollow, with useable flakes and possibly partially worked cores being removed for use and further knapping elsewhere. It probably represents, therefore the debris from one or more knapping events that was gathered up and disposed of, rather than *in situ* knapping.

While there was no direct evidence for Middle Bronze Age cultivation on the site, for instance in the form of field boundaries, an accumulation of colluvium in the base of a dry valley at the west of the site may indicate erosion caused by local clearance and cultivation in this period. The colluvium was recorded for 600 m along the southern edge of Area B, with a maximum width of 50 m and depth of 1.6 m. The date of its inception is uncertain. It appears to post-date Middle Bronze Age roundhouse B49 but a spread of burnt flint of possible Late Bronze Age/Early Iron Age date (below) sealed an intermittent colluvial deposit (206), up to 0.2 m deep, containing four fragments of Deverel-Rimbury pottery (Fig. 7, 4). Analysis of a monolith taken through the colluvium identified different episodes of colluviation, with evidence of soil formation in the lower colluvium suggesting a period of stability. The upper levels of the colluvium could be considerably later, perhaps post-dating the Late Bronze Age Wessex Linear Ditch (below) and possibly even contemporary with lynchets in the area that are considered to be of Romano-British date (below).

Figure 9 Comparative plans of post-built roundhouses and six-post structure

Burnt Flint Features

The pattern of settlement and agriculture established during the Middle Bronze Age appears to have reached its peak during the Early Iron Age, but there was little direct evidence for distinctly Late Bronze Age activity. A number of sherds of transitional Middle/Late Bronze Age pottery were recovered from Area A East and Area D, but only a few sherds from the site are certainly derived from Late Bronze Age vessels, such as from roundhouse F7202 (above).

One radiocarbon date, however, calibrated to 900–810 cal BC (KIA-34936 95%; 2685±25 BP), falls within the Late Bronze Age. This was obtained from a piece of oak roundwood charcoal from a rectangular, east-west aligned pit (D5562) in Area D North (Fig. 22). The pit was at least 2.5 m long, 1 m wide, and 0.3 m deep, with vertical sides and a flat base, and its upper fill consisted entirely of burnt flint and charcoal, dominated by oak. This feature was one of a number of apparently non-domestic features recorded across the site characterised by large quantities of burnt flint. Some 20 m to its south-east, two parallel east-west slots (D5833 and D5834), also filled with burnt flint and charcoal, may be associated with the pit, although they too are of unknown function. The slots were both at least 1.0 m long and 1.4 m apart, and the northern slot had a small pit or post-hole at its west end, also filled with burnt flint.

Some 300 m to the south-west, a large amorphous feature (E5204), possibly a series of pits or natural hollows, again containing burnt flint, was recorded during the evaluation of Area E (Fig. 3). The feature, measuring at least 17 x 9 m and 1.1 m deep, contained a silty clay fill with moderate quantities of burnt flint and lesser amounts of charcoal, as well as some lenses of burnt flint. Although it produced no dating evidence, the presence of such large quantities of burnt flint probably suggests a later prehistoric date.

Another extensive layer of burnt flint (B14205) was exposed in a series of test-pits in the base of a dry valley at the south-west corner of Area B (Fig. 3). It extended at least 25 m west to east (but not into Area C west of Sherborne Road) and a similar distance north to south, being thickest (0.25 m) to the west. Although dark in colour, it contained few identifiable charcoal fragments. It overlay an intermittent colluvial deposit containing Deverel-Rimbury pottery (Fig. 7, 4) and itself contained a further abraded sherd and a flint flake, but produced no other dating evidence, although it was sealed by further colluvium, at this point up to 1.0 m thick.

The location of this burnt flint spread, like the features in Area D, in the base of a valley, and the Area E flint spread in a north-facing coombe, suggests that all these features containing burnt flint may originally have been sited close to water. While the single radiocarbon date from pit D5562 places that feature within the Late Bronze Age, the other features containing burnt flint are undated, although mounds or spreads of burnt flint close to water are a relatively common feature within the Middle and Late Bronze Age. These features, although of uncertain function, appear to indicate some form of localised but repeated burning activity, possibly involving the heating of water (Barfield 1991), whether for industrial, domestic, or other social/ritual purposes.

Discussion

The contrast in the character of the evidence for Middle Bronze Age activity with that from the preceding periods is marked, indicating major changes in settlement patterns and economic practices. The pattern of open settlement indicated by the evidence from Areas A, D, and F has parallels elsewhere in Hampshire such as at Winnall Down (Fasham 1985), Easton Lane (Fasham et al. 1989), and Westbury West Meon (Lewis and Walker 1977).

The archaeological visibility of the early roundhouses indicates more substantial and probably more permanent domestic structures than those previously constructed, reflecting the requirements of an economy within which arable cultivation was probably playing a far greater role. The possibility (in Area D) of contemporary burials close to the settlement adds to the picture of a more sedentary society, developing a new relationship with the landscape. The absence of hazelnuts with the domestic refuse suggests a far greater emphasis on food production rather than procurement by this period, and although hulled wheat, either spelt, or emmer, is the only cereal recognised, weeds typical of arable activity were also recorded. While no field boundaries or enclosures were identified, Deverel-Rimbury pottery was possibly associated with an onset of colluviation within a dry valley at the west of the site.

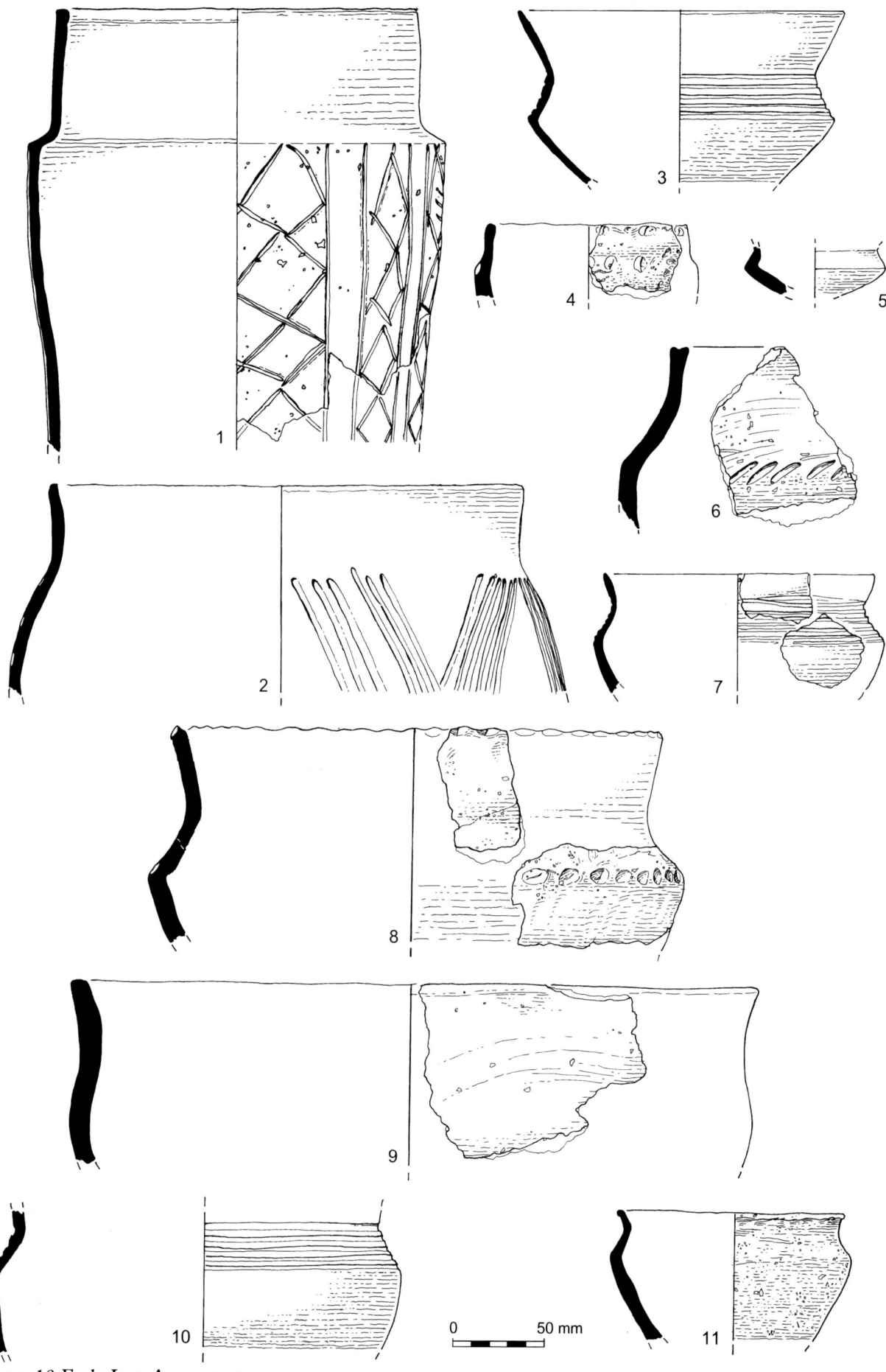

Figure 10 Early Iron Age pottery

Early Iron Age

By the Early Iron Age there was an extensive open settlement, comprising at least 10 roundhouses, strung out along the chalk ridge in Areas A South and East and Area F (Fig. 3). Of the 665 sherds of pottery (6111 g) that can be described as belonging to the Late Bronze Age/Early Iron Age or Early Iron Age, most of the assemblage (Fig. 10, 1–11), in particular from Areas A South and East and F, can be placed within the earliest or Early Iron Age as defined by Cunliffe (1991) and, more specifically for Hampshire and Wiltshire, by Brown (2000). It includes bipartite vessels and tripartite jars and bowls, manufactured from a range of predominantly flint- or sand-tempered fabrics, and is similar to assemblages from other sites within the Basingstoke area, most notably the earlier pottery from Winklebury (Smith 1977) and Cowdery's Down (Thompson 1983), to the small assemblage from Brighton Hill South (Morris 1992) and further afield Winnall Down (Hawkes 1985, 61–2, figs 52–3). Such assemblages are generally thought to be no earlier than the late 8th or 7th century BC and with a currency that lasted until the 6th century BC.

Area A South

There was a significant focus of Early Iron Age settlement in Area A South, in a relatively elevated position on the chalk ridge (Figs 3 and 11). It comprised four roundhouses, two of them replaced by later structures in approximately the same positions, possible fence-lines, isolated pits, and a probable four-post structure.

Two of the overlapping roundhouses were sited towards the north-west of the area and although one post-hole (A55328) had been used in both structures it was not possible to determine which structure was built first (Fig. 9). Roundhouse A55630 comprised a circle, 6.2 m in diameter, of ten, mostly evenly spaced, undated post-holes, with a wider (2.9 m) gap at the east-south-east indicating the entrance. Its south-eastern side was overlapped by the north-western side of roundhouse A55631, which also had ten post-holes and was only slightly larger at 6.7 m diameter. Again, a wider (2.8 m) gap at the east-south-east indicates the entrance. Post-holes at the south-west of the circle

Figure 11 Prehistoric features in Area A South

produced a small assemblage of Early Iron Age pottery (some of it burnt), animal bone, and worked and burnt flint. Neither structure had any evidence of a porch.

In contrast, the two overlapping roundhouses towards the centre of the area were very different in size, the smaller structure (A55293), at 6.1 m in diameter, being similar in scale to the two to the north-west (see Fig. 2.11), but the large structure (A55293), at 11.1 m in diameter, being the largest of all the roundhouses recorded during the excavations (Fig. 9). Although two of the post-holes appeared to have been used in both structures, it was again not possible to tell, from that evidence alone, which was the earlier structure.

The smaller roundhouse (A55293) had nine post-holes, and although the widest gap was at the north-east, this may mark the position of a truncated post-hole; the gap at the south-east, although only 1.6 m wide, was flanked by two of the largest post-holes and is the more usual location for the entrance. The only Early Iron Age pottery came from one of the post-holes (A55224) shared with the larger roundhouse, along with burnt flint and animal bone; two other post-holes (A55358 and A55362) produced intrusive fragments of Late Iron Age/early Romano-British pottery.

The smaller roundhouse lay within the southern half of the larger roundhouse (A55292), which was defined by 20 post-holes with quite variable spacing, some less than 1.0 m apart, possibly indicating repairs, but others over 3.0 m apart at the west and north (Fig. 9). Given the surviving depths of the post-holes at c. 0.3–0.4 m, it is unlikely that many had been lost through truncation, so it is possible that these gaps represent additional entrances, although in atypical positions. The south side of the western gap was flanked by two external post-holes (A55303 and A55305), although these may not be directly associated with the roundhouse. The most likely position for the main entrance is the 2.7 m wide gap just south of east, 3.2 m outside of which were two large oval post-holes (A55308 and A55606) forming a possible porch, although the only pottery from A55308 was a single sherd of presumably residual Middle Bronze Age pottery. Other artefacts, comprising Early Iron Age pottery, burnt flint, and small fragments of burnt animal bone were retrieved from post-holes mainly on the southern side of the roundhouse.

Immediately south-east of this pair of roundhouses was a line of substantial post-holes (Fig. 9), possibly aligned on the front the porch of A55292; one (A55607) contained a sherd of Early Iron Age pottery and burnt flint. To their west was an irregular group of smaller post-holes, including one close pair, three evenly spaced in a line, and one cut by a short linear slot; all were undated. There were other post-holes in the area around the four roundhouses, many of which were undated but possibly contemporary with them (or with the Late Iron Age/early Romano-British enclosure, below). While some were isolated features, others appeared to occur in groups, suggesting some structural or functional association. A group of three post-holes (A55619), spaced 2.5 m apart, could have formed two sides of a four-post structure whose fourth post-hole was destroyed by the later enclosure ditch (below); one of the post-holes contained Early Iron Age pottery, burnt flint, and copious large fragments of wood charcoal (mature oak) indicative of a post that had been burnt *in situ*. Another loose group of post-holes, some 20 m south of the roundhouses, included three (A55371, A55387, and A55391), spaced 4.2 m and 5.4 m apart and all containing Early Iron Age pottery, which may have formed two sides of a another small sub-square structure (others in the group appeared to form a Late Iron Age/early Romano-British structure (below).

Area A East

The greatest concentration of settlement evidence in this period was recorded in Area A East, some 400 m to the east-north-east of the large roundhouse in Area A South, and at a lower level along the chalk ridge (Figs 3 and 7). This included two (possibly four) roundhouses, one of which had been rebuilt, other possible post-built structures, a series of fence-lines, and an extensive area of intercutting pits.

The two phases of the rebuilt roundhouse (A50029/A50100) had internal diameters of 9.5 m and 8.9 m, respectively, although here too it was not possible to establish which was built first (Fig. 9). Most of the post-holes could be assigned to one or other phase, although four at the north and east could have belonged to either phase, or both; two large porch post-holes, 1.6 m apart and 1–2 m outside the rings at the east-south-east, were also apparently reused. The smaller phase of construction (A50100) comprised least 18 post-holes, the deepest (up to 0.46 m) being at the south-east. Over 250 g of Early Iron Age pottery, some of it heat-damaged, was recovered from five of the six post-holes south-west of the entrance and from one opposite the entrance (Fig. 12). Burnt flint was recovered in the same areas, and a flint hammerstone was recovered from opposite the entrance. Such distributions of artefacts may reflect different areas of activity inside the roundhouse, influenced in part by the availability of natural light. While the heat-damaged pottery might indicate that the building had burnt down, no fired clay, a likely by-

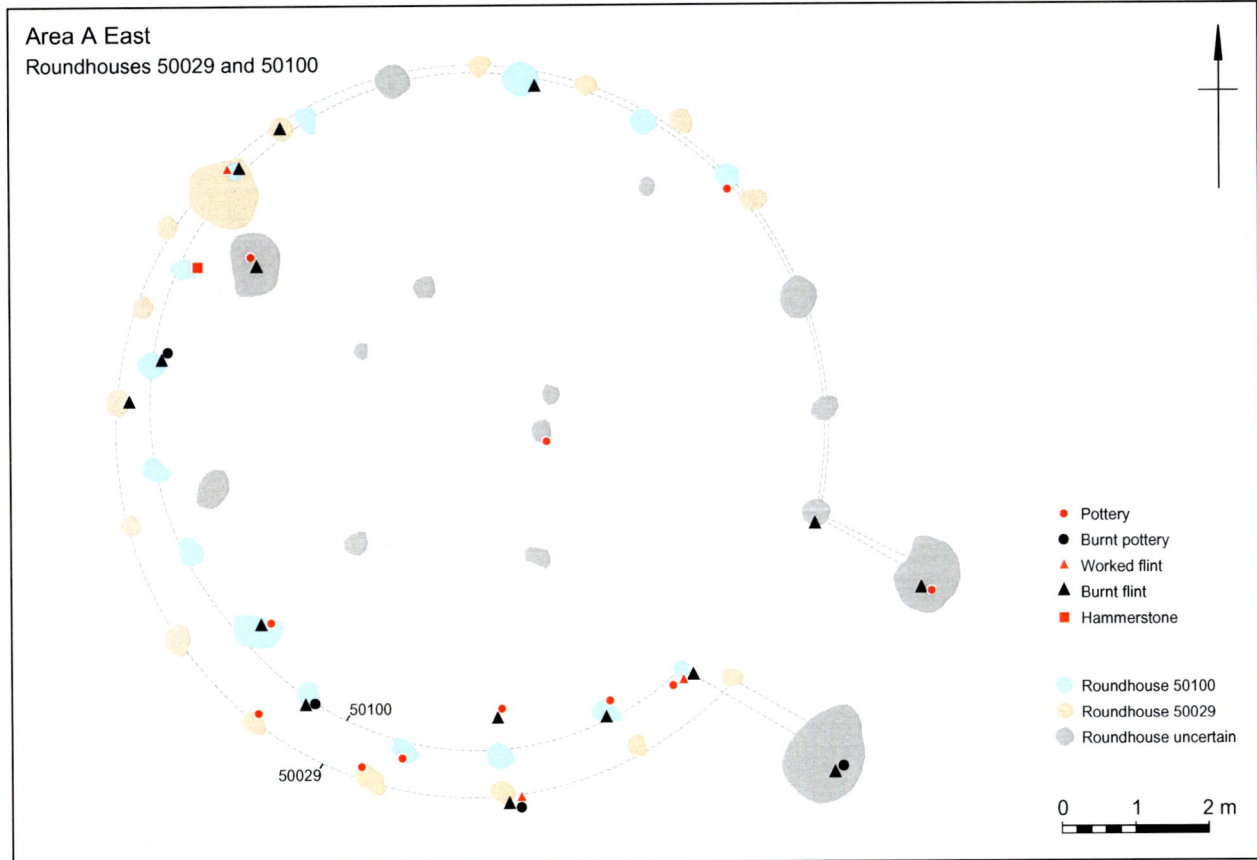

Figure 12 Detailed plan of roundhouses A50029 and A50100 showing the distribution of selected finds

product of a wattle-built house, was recovered either from the post-holes, or from an adjacent broad hollow (A50197 below), comprising a group of intercutting pits which also contained burnt pottery. This hollow, if broadly contemporary with roundhouse A50100, might have been the natural place for such burnt debris to accumulate.

The larger phase (A50029) of the roundhouse's construction comprised probably 19 post-holes, those at the south-east and south being deeper (up to 0.4 m). Most of the finds, comprising *c*. 200 g of Early Iron Age pottery (some again heat-damaged), small quantities of burnt flint, fired clay, and fragments of animal bone, were recovered from the post-holes on the south side (Fig. 12). One (A50155) of the seven post-holes near the centre of the roundhouse), contained fragments of Early Iron Age pottery, but while these features may represent internal supports they formed no obvious pattern. There were also two shallow pits on the west side, one containing further pottery, although these need not have been contemporary with the roundhouse; a third pit, at the north-west, lay on the line of the post-holes and was cut by one of those of the smaller phase of construction.

A similar roundhouse (A50101) lay 35 m to the west-north-west. It comprised an 8.7 m diameter ring of 14 evenly spaced post-holes, with a 3.0 m wide gap on the east-south-east side, where there was a splayed porch of four large post-holes extending out *c*. 2.5 m (Fig. 9). Early Iron Age pottery (some, here too, heat-damaged) was recovered from two post-holes at the south-west and from two of the porch post-holes; fragments of fired clay were retrieved at the south, while burnt flint was more evenly distributed.

Further groups of post-holes in Area A East, although undated, may represent contemporary structures. At the north-east, there was an oval setting, *c*. 5.3 m wide and 5.8 m deep, of ten post-holes (A50432); an irregular arrangement of four post-holes outside the 3.2 m gap at the south-east, may represent an entrance porch, but this is far from clear (Fig. 9). A small modern metal rod found in one of the post-holes is likely to be intrusive. Towards the north-west, five unevenly spaced post-holes (A50196), 1.5–3.2 m apart, formed an irregular arc on the eastern and southern side of a possible circle with a projected diameter of *c*. 8.0 m. There was a further post-hole off centre within the arc. While this too may represent the remains of a truncated roundhouse (Fig. 9), there was no porch, and if the post-holes were associated they may have formed some other type of structure of unknown function.

There were also two possible four-post structures. Structure A50268, south of possible roundhouse A50196, measured 2.2–2.5 x 3.5 m; perhaps less convincingly was the slightly diamond-shaped post setting (A50370) south-west of roundhouse A50432, which had sides averaging 2.6 m, a sample from which produced two indeterminate cereal grains and one glume base (identified as spelt/emmer wheat). Similar features are often interpreted as granaries, and if these groups represent genuine structures, they probably belong with the Early Iron Age phase of occupation, despite an absence of diagnostic artefacts.

A number of fence-lines were also recorded in Area A East, passing between some of the roundhouses and appearing to divide up the settlement into blocks (Fig. 6). The most regular was a c. 20 m long line (A50195) of 10 relatively evenly spaced post-holes (average spacing 2.1 m), whose west-north-west to east-south-east alignment closely matches the orientations of the roundhouses. As they became both smaller and shallower to the west-north-west, where truncation was heaviest, the fence probably continued further in that direction. A slightly less regular, 19 m long line of seven post-holes (A50328), lay almost parallel to, and 45 m to the south-west of, fence-line A50195. The post-hole at the western end (A50307) was angled at c. 30° from vertical towards the fence, there being a gap of 4.7 m to the next post (A50329), compared to the average spacing of 2.8 m for the other posts. Three slightly larger post-holes, running in a line for 11 m to the south-west (and probably beyond the excavation area) may have formed another fence-line, or, with A50328, defined the corner of a partial enclosure, which the angled post-hole lay outside. A number of the post-holes contained small quantities of worked and burnt flint, but no pottery, although it is reasonable to associate the fence-lines with the roundhouses. The irregular line of 14 post-holes (A50443) running west from possible Middle Bronze Age structure A50199 (above) may also belong to this phase, as may an group of further undated post-holes to its south which form no recognisable structure and are of unknown function.

Two large irregular features, originally interpreted as working hollows, were recorded near roundhouse A50029/A50100. The larger (A50197), up to 13 m wide, was shown (in a 1.2 m wide excavated slot) to comprise a cluster of intercutting and heavily weathered pits, each up to 2 m wide and 0.3 m deep. The similarity of their fills, combined with subsequent animal disturbance, precluded their detailed analysis, but together they produced 332 sherds of Middle Bronze Age and Early Iron Age pottery (and residual earlier sherds), worked flint (257 pieces), burnt flint (55 pieces), animal bone (29) including horse, cattle, and sheep/goat, as well as pieces of antler, fired clay (5), and a single piece of probable non-local stone. As most of the flints were of Late Neolithic date (above) it appears that one or more earlier feature was partially destroyed during the digging of these pits. The pottery from these pits included at least three freshly broken but incomplete Early Iron Age vessels (Fig. 10, 1–3), including a jar with complex decoration, a furrowed bowl, and a globular jar. The smaller feature (A50445), measuring c. 2.0 x 3.0 m, appeared to comprise four pits and produced a further 40 Early Iron Age sherds, 32 pieces of worked flint, and 7 pieces of burnt flint. A 4.0 m long gully (A50230) of unknown function, lying north-west of the larger pit group, contained Early Iron Age pottery, and worked and burnt flint.

Area F

A roundhouse (F7169), on the east side of Chineham Lane, clearly forms part of the same focus of settlement recorded in Area A East (Fig. 6). It lay to the immediate south of possible Middle Bronze Age roundhouse F7202 (above), and comprised an 11 m diameter circle of 15 relatively evenly-spaced post-holes, with a 2.2 m wide entrance porch, comprising a further three post-holes, facing just south of east (Fig. 9). The inner two post-holes of the porch were larger than the third, outer one, and it is possible that the missing (fourth) outer post-hole had been truncated. Early Iron Age pottery (and one residual Late Bronze Age sherd) was recovered from post-holes along the south- to south-west arc of the roundhouse, and the inner pair of porch post-holes contained over 2 kg of burnt flint. The only internal features were two shallow possible post-holes. A single radiocarbon date (KIA-37132; 2430±25 BP 95%) was obtained on a fragment of charred sloe stone from post-hole F7134 and when calibrated falls within the Early Iron Age: 750-400 cal BC. There was a contemporary pit (F7067) just north of the roundhouse (within possible Middle Bronze Age roundhouse F7202; Fig. 9); it contained almost 0.5 kg of Early Iron Age pottery, single pieces of worked flint and non-local stone, burnt flint and fragments of animal bone. A radiocarbon date of 750–410 cal BC was obtained from a charred barley grain (KIA-37131; 2449±25 BP 95%).

Three short lengths of shallow, undated gully north-west of the roundhouse may be associated with it (or possibly with Middle Bronze Age roundhouse F7202). Two lengths (F7117 and F7118), up to 0.6 m wide and separated by a 0.8 m wide gap, ran north-east to south-west for 8 m before turning to the south-south-east for a further 1.0 m, while the third (F7078), up to 1.0 m wide and with a similar alignment, was cut by a tree-throw hole, which contained small and worn fragments, probably residual, of Middle Neolithic Peterborough Ware pottery (above).

Other structures in Area F included an 8.5 m diameter roundhouse (F7201) 120 m to the south-east of roundhouse F7169, in Area F3. This comprised 13 post-holes in a circle, with a further two porch post-holes, 2 m apart at the south-east, 1.0 m outside the circle (Fig. 9), one of which produced Early Iron Age pottery. It was unclear whether two other post-holes, one inside the other just outside the roundhouse, were related to it.

There was also a rectangular structure of at least six post-holes (F7199) in Area F1; this may have continued west of the excavation area. It comprised at least three pairs of post-holes in two almost parallel rows, forming an irregular rectangle c. 4.3 m long and 2.5 m wide (Fig. 9). Early Iron Age pottery, some heat damaged, was recovered from five of the post-holes, along with a small number of worked flints and 400 g of burnt flint. The structure is of unknown function, although two pits to its immediate east may be associated with it; one of these (F6303) contained part of a small furrowed bowl and a single piece of worked flint, the other (F6305) contained 62 sherds (698 g) of Early Iron Age pottery (including from a number of plain and fingertip impressed jars), worked and burnt flint, featureless fired clay, and fragments of unidentifiable animal bone.

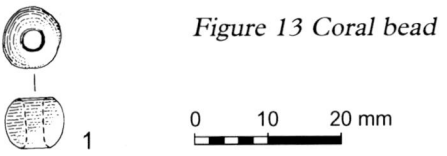

Figure 13 Coral bead

The area between the excavated structures in Area F revealed few other features during the evaluation of the site, and were consequently not subject to area excavation. However, given the apparent isolation, particularly of roundhouse F7201 (in Area F3), it is reasonable to assume that there were other contemporary features, such as further roundhouses, fence-lines, and pits more widely distributed within the unexcavated areas particularly along the top and on the south facing slope of the chalk ridge. A number of other more isolated Early Iron Age pits and post-holes were recorded in the area and while some appear to occur in pairs, overall they show no other pattern in their distribution. These included a pit (F7038), in Area F1, whose primary fill was recut (7040) and hearth material, including 1870 g of burnt flint, dumped in the recut, as well as a coral bead (Fig. 13). In addition, a number of Late Bronze Age/Early Iron Age pits and post-holes had been previously recorded 270 m east of roundhouse F7201, at Chineham Lane (Boismier *et al.* 1998; Fig. 2).

Near the far north-eastern edge of Area F (in Area F5), an arc of four post-holes (F8318) may represent the truncated remains of a further roundhouse (Figs 3 and 9), 300 m north-north-east of the nearest contemporary roundhouse. The post-holes, two of which contained Early Iron Age pottery, were spaced 1.8–2.7 m apart and formed the south-eastern quadrant of a circle 8.5 m in diameter. Unlike those to the south-west, it was located towards the base of the chalk ridge on its northern side, indicating that the settlement may have been more extensive within the landscape than is suggested by the distribution of the other roundhouses which were sited predominantly on the ridge.

Landscape Division

The extensive occupation of the landscape appears to have been accompanied by a level of formal division and organisation not previously encountered on the site. While small-scale, local boundaries are suggested by fence-lines within the settlement areas, possibly from the Middle Bronze Age, the wider organisation of the landscape is most clearly indicated by two substantial ditches, interpreted as Wessex Linear ditches (Fig. 3). The course of one ditch ran approximately west-south-west to east-north-east along the southern edge of the chalk ridge, just above the base of the dry valley. The other, running perpendicular to it for over 300 m, cut across the eastern end of the ridge in Area F, defining the eastern end of the area of settlement, with the exception of the low-lying possible roundhouse in Area F5. The ditches probably converged just beyond the limits of the site, possibly being comparable, therefore, to the arrangement of spinal and subsidiary ditches that are particularly well preserved on Salisbury Plain (Bradley *et al.* 1994; McOmish *et al.* 2002), which divided up the landscape into blocks of different scale.

The east-west ditch (B7/C1) was observed for c. 1.2 km following a slightly meandering course across Areas B and C. Towards its western end it turned up the slope in a series of steps appearing to avoid an earlier feature (see above), there being a narrow (1.0 m) break at this point (Fig. 5). Wessex Linear ditches often run close to earlier burial monuments (McOmish *et al.* 2002, 64–5), and one on Chapperton Down, Salisbury Plain, also made a series of turns, suggesting a similar deliberate avoidance of some pre-existing feature (*ibid.*, fig. 3.15). Although ditch B7/C1 was heavily truncated in the eastern part of Area C, in areas where it was protected by overlying colluvium it was up to 2.5 m wide and 1.1 m deep with a V-shaped profile, a calcareous primary fill and,

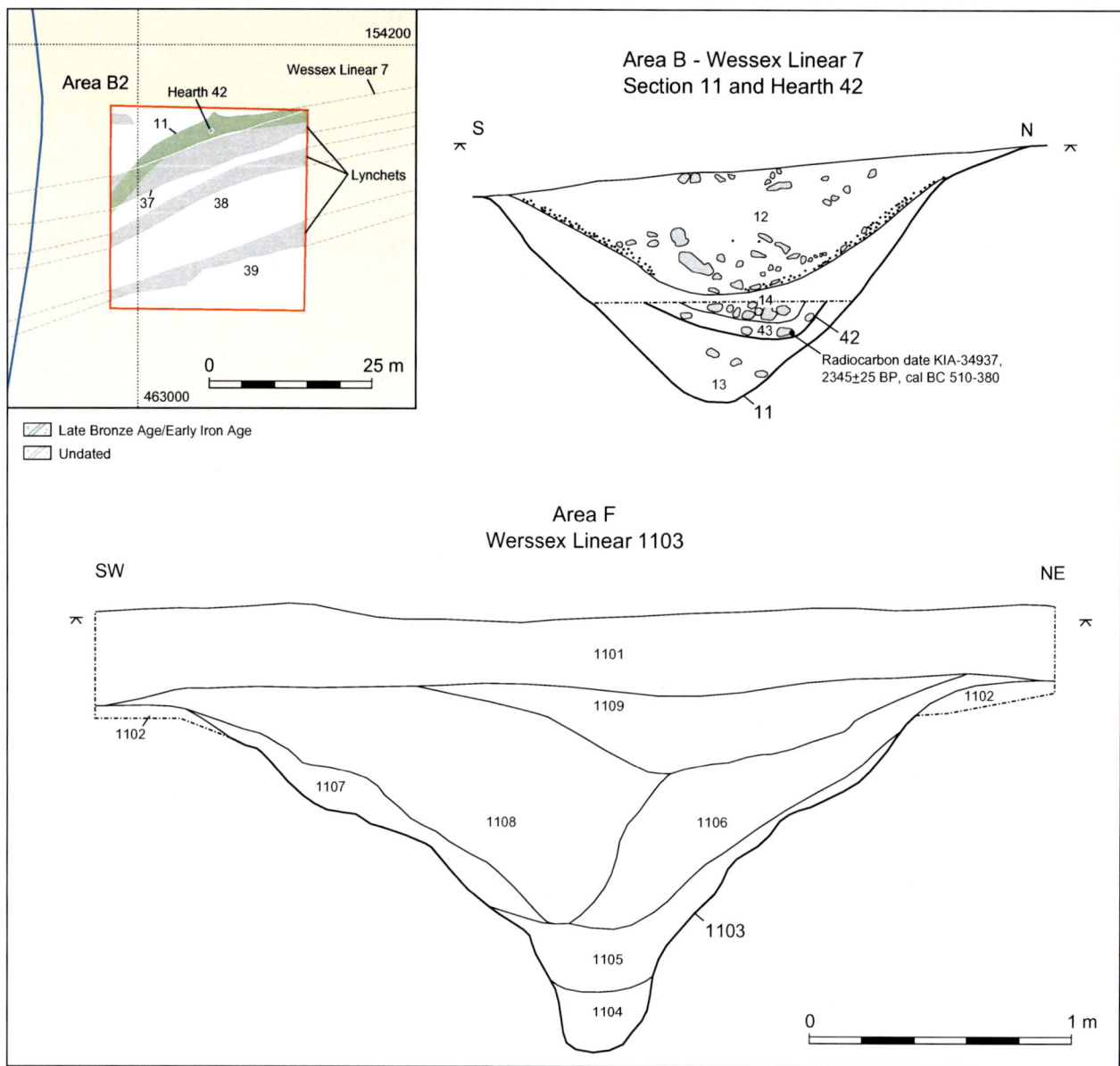

Figure 14 Areas B and F: Wessex Linear ditches, sections and inset plan of Area B2 showing hearth

in some interventions, a secondary fill and a looser ploughwash-derived tertiary fill in places containing a high concentration of flint nodules (Fig. 14).

Analysis of molluscs from ditch B7/C1 indicates the existence of trees rather than a hedgerow nearby, which could also help account for the ditch's irregular alignment. More of these trees may have cleared when the ditch was being maintained, the immediate landscape being generally open grassland and, by the time the ditch was abandoned, the landscape appears to have become both more open and stable. The presence of large flint nodules in the upper fill may represents a change from pasture to arable cultivation at some later date, later than an Early Iron Age hearth in Area B2 (Fig. 14) and possibly during the Romano-British period (see below).

A number of features parallel to the ditch may have been associated with it, including another ditch (B3/C11) on its northern side, 1.1 m wide and 0.7 m deep, which contained pottery of Late Bronze Age-Early Iron Age date and worked flints. Parallel features to the south (Figs 14 and 27), including negative lynchets and possible hedge-lines (B37–39 and C8–10), were of uncertain date, producing finds, some possibly intrusive, of Romano-British, medieval, and post-medieval date. There appeared to be a greater concentration of tree-throw holes on the north side of the ditch and, while this may reflect differences in landuse, it is possible that negative lynchets below the ditch had truncated some of these features.

The north-south Wessex Linear ditch, towards its southern end (F1103; Fig. 3), was 3.1 m wide and up to 1.3 m deep with moderately steep sides and a narrow, steep-sided slot in the base (Fig. 14), but became progressively narrower towards the north, where it was only 1.2 m wide. It produced Early Iron

Age pottery, worked and burnt flint, and a piece of sandstone, possibly a fragment of a quernstone.

The profiles of the ditch, the fills, and their low levels of artefacts are all typical of Wessex Linear ditches, making their precise dating problematic (Bradley et al. 1994). While small quantities of Late Bronze Age pottery were recovered, most of the well-stratified and more complete vessel profiles belong in the Early Iron Age, more specifically the 7th–6th centuries BC. An excavated section of the east-west ditch in Area B2 exposed an oval hearth deposit (B42), cut 0.15 m into ditch's lower fill and filled largely with charcoal and some burnt flint (Fig. 14). A radiocarbon determination on a single sample of charcoal pomaccons fruitwood recovered from the hearth deposit gave a date in the Early Iron Age of 510–380 cal BC (95% 2345±25 BP; KIA-34937). This indicates that the ditch was constructed by at least the 5th century and possibly the 6th century, although it could have been earlier, possibly dating to the later Bronze Age. However, some Wessex Linear ditches are known to have been partly recut in the Late Iron Age and Romano-British periods, possibly accounting for the presence of sherds of Middle/Late Bronze Age, Early/Middle Iron Age, Late Iron Age/early Romano-British, and Romano-British date, as well as quantities of worked and burnt flint and a Romano-British hobnail.

Discussion

The period spanning the Late Bronze Age and Early Iron Age saw both the intensification and the expansion of the earlier settlement along the chalk ridge; Winklebury, at the western end of the ridge, was also densely occupied by this period (Smith 1977). Unfortunately it was not possible to determine exactly how the settlements on the site developed, although the presence of fence-lines within the Area A East settlement might indicate divisions within an extended settlement rather that a shifting sequence of individual roundhouses. Similarly, while it was not possible to determine the order in which the overlapping small and large roundhouses in Area A South were constructed, it is not unreasonable to suppose that the larger structure was a replacement, built on a grander scale. If so, there appears to have been a significant increase in the sizes of roundhouses during this period (Fig. 9). The Middle Bronze Age roundhouses (with the exception of B49) and three of the Early Iron Age roundhouses in Area A South averaged c. 6.0 m in diameter. A further six structures were 8.0–9.5 m in diameter and two were 11 m, indicating probably both advances in construction technique and social changes. The addition of external porches to roundhouses in the Early Iron Age, as well as having functional uses, represents the elaboration of the entrance, enhancing the appearance of the building and making a statement about it occupants' status.

Not only was there an intensification of settlement in this period but there was also the first evidence for the formal division of the landscape, with boundaries of different kinds laid out at varying scales within it. However, the low levels of both plant remains and animal bones recovered from Late Bronze Age/Early Iron Age features hamper the analysis of agricultural landuse during this period. The dominance of oak in the charcoal in Late Bronze Age pit D5562, at least half of which was of roundwood cut at 2–4 years, suggests the use of managed, probably coppiced oak stands as a fuel source. The mollusc analysis from one of the Wessex Linear Ditches, however, may indicate an increasingly cleared and grassed landscape, possibly reflecting the importance of animal husbandry in the economy – cattle, sheep/goat, and horse bones, for example, being recovered from the pits in Area A East. It is possible that these ditches had some agricultural role, such as marking 'ranch boundaries', in addition to social and political roles in defining territorial divisions (Bowen 1978). The ditches were regularly maintained with little chalk rubble forming a primary fill and they would have formed a substantial obstacle, particularly to cattle. The charcoal in the Early Iron Age hearth deposit close to the base of the ditch was dominated by hawthorn type wood indicative of scrub or hedgerows. The positioning of the ditches may also have been related to different areas of activity as they appear to separate the area of settlement from previously used areas containing a variety of burnt mound and burnt flint-rich features.

Late Iron Age/Romano-British

Following the Early Iron Age settlement, there is little evidence from the site for activity in the late 6th–5th centuries and, as no Middle Iron Age features were recorded, it is possible that settlement shifted either towards a possible banjo enclosure recognised from aerial photographs, further up the ridge 300 m west of Area A (Fig. 3), or to a circular enclosure at Oakridge, c. 1 km south of Area D (Perry 1970, 43; Oliver 1992). The establishment of the hillfort at Winklebury, c. 2 km to the south-west of Popley (Fig. 2), in the Middle Iron Age further reflects changes in the settlement pattern in this period and a new emphasis on enclosed settlement. The Merton Rise/Marnel Park site was not occupied again until around the time of the Roman Conquest.

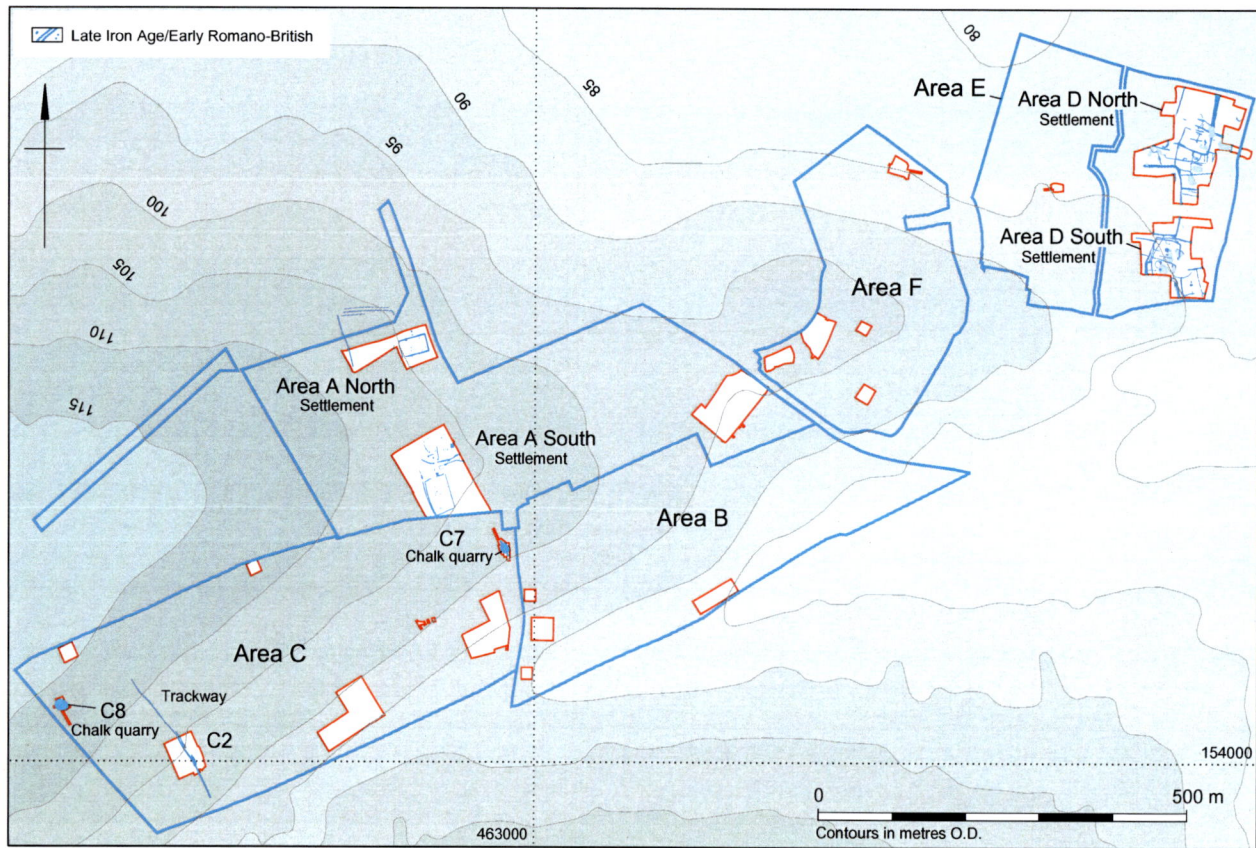

Figure 15 Distribution of Late Iron Age/Romano-British features

The Late Iron Age would also have been a period of significant change for the native population in the Basingstoke area, with the establishment of the Atrebatic capital 6 km to the north at Silchester (*Calleva*), and the associated centralisation of power that had formerly been dispersed at hillfort sites (Fig. 2). Winklebury was abandoned in the 1st century BC (Smith 1977). In contrast, there may have been a strong element of continuity in the lives of the native population in the immediate pre-Roman Conquest and post-Conquest periods. In many material respects, the upper strata of Late Iron Age society were already highly romanised by AD 43, with evidence at Silchester for the importation from the continent of wine, olive oil, and other luxury products. While some of these influences would have filtered down to the rural communities occupying dispersed downland farmsteads, many elements of the native Iron Age rural culture, such as house construction, agricultural practices, and pottery styles, continued little changed into the early Romano-British period and beyond.

At Marnel Park and Merton Rise, the Late Iron Age/Romano-British settlements, with associated enclosures, fields, and trackways, were concentrated in Areas A and D (Fig. 15); in addition, quarries and a trackway were recorded in Area C and there is evidence for field lynchets and re-use of an Iron Age boundary ditch in Area B. The pottery fabrics and vessel forms indicate that activity was well-established by the middle of the 1st century AD, if not before, continuing on into the 4th, possibly even early 5th centuries.

Areas A South and North

Areas A South (Fig. 16) and North (Fig. 19) contained a range of features – a trackway, enclosures, structures, possible wells, gullies, and pits – arranged across the site in a way that suggests a coherent and integrated organisation of the landscape. Once established it underwent little change during what the pottery assemblage suggests was a relatively brief occupation. There were relatively few contexts where the potentially Late Iron Age fabrics – the grog-tempered, early sandy, and flint-tempered Silchester-type wares – occurred alone in any quantity without other more characteristically Romanised wares, perhaps suggesting a start date spanning the Conquest period.

Area A South

A short, *c.* 3.7 m wide trackway in Area A South approached from the east-north-east, where the ditches that bounded it splayed out to form a wide funnel, possibly to aid in the control and movement of livestock. A north-south line of four post-holes, lying across the mouth of the funnel, may indicate the position of gates or a similar movable barrier. The ditches on the north side (A55636/7 and 55642/6), which had been extended and recut on at least one occasion, had a 4.0 m wide entrance gap. While the size of the ditch (1.3 m wide and 0.5 m deep), and its curving line give it the appearance of an enclosure ditch, it ran for only *c.* 50 m, and appears, therefore, to have formed only a localised barrier, separating the trackway from a group of features and structures to its north. Substantial quantities of apparently domestic refuse, however, had been dumped in the ditch, comprising animal bone (including fragmentary cattle skulls), burnt clay, burnt flint, and pottery including, from near the western terminal, the complete profile of a beaded rim jar. The pottery assemblage contained numerous complete and semi-complete vessel profiles which (together with a Silchester-type ware lid from pit A55458 in Area A North, below) typifies the range of mid–late 1st century AD fabrics and forms from this part of the site (Fig. 17, 1–11). The inclusion of human skull fragments within the dumped material suggest its deposition at this location may have had been of partly symbolic significance rather than being just a matter of expediency.

A possible well (A55101) was located immediately inside the ditch entrance on its eastern side (Fig. 18). It was 1.6 m in diameter, with shallow sides tapering to a 1.0 m diameter vertical shaft at a depth of *c.* 0.3 m. Excavation stopped at 1.2 m, but probing indicated that it continued to at least 1.7 m. It contained early Romano-British pottery, a chalk spindlewhorl (Fig. 18), burnt clay, burnt and worked flint, shell, and fragments from a cattle skull. A single possible post-hole on the north side of the feature may be associated with it. A gully (55643) ran north from the well petering out after *c.* 18 m, possibly forming an internal division within the area north of the trackway and aligned approximately on the entrance.

Within Area A South there were four square post-built structures, averaging 2.3 m square. Five-post structure A55542 and four-post structures A55574 and A55659 were undated, but four-post structure A55597 produced single sherds of both Late Bronze

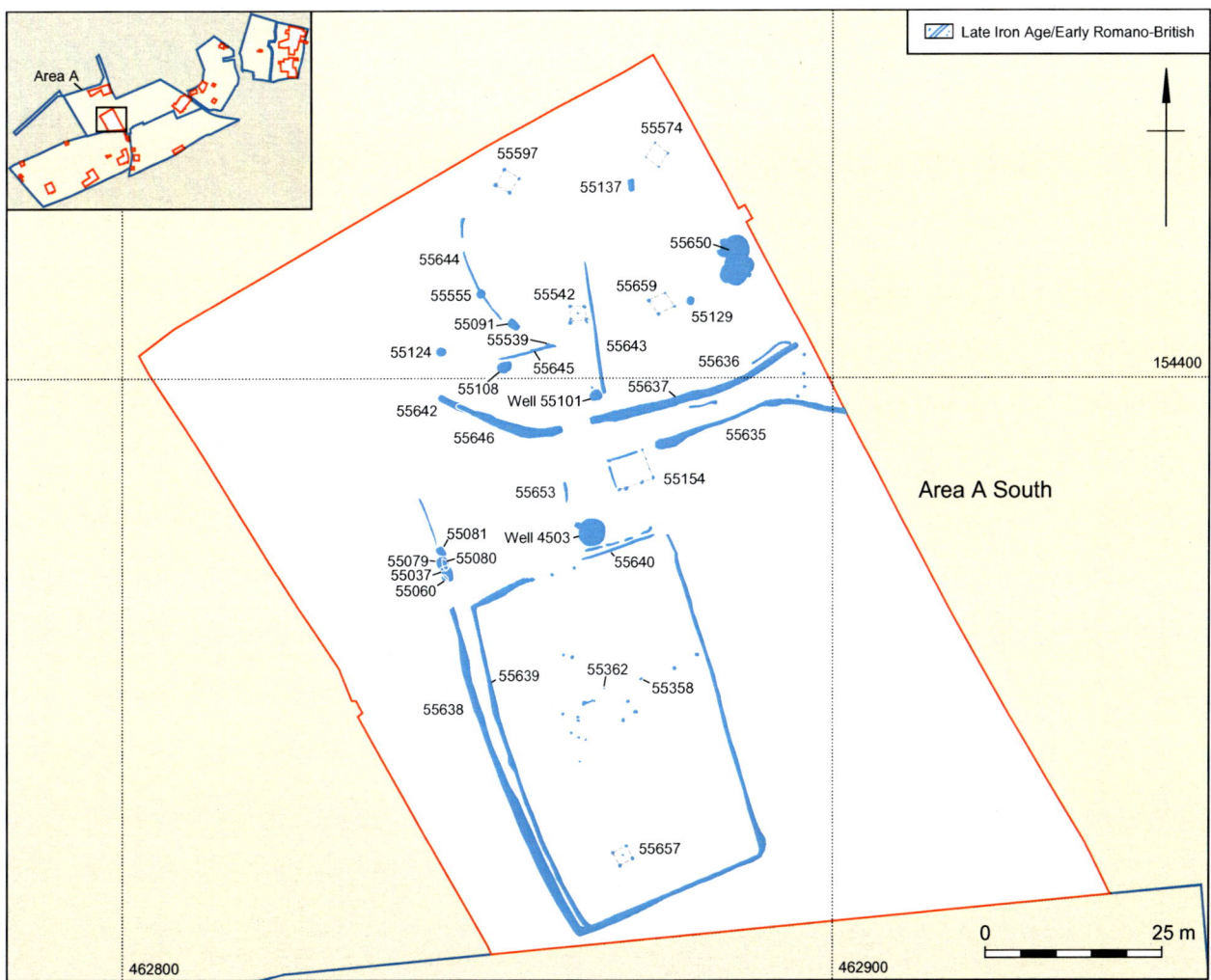

Figure 16 Late Iron Age/Romano-British features in Area A South

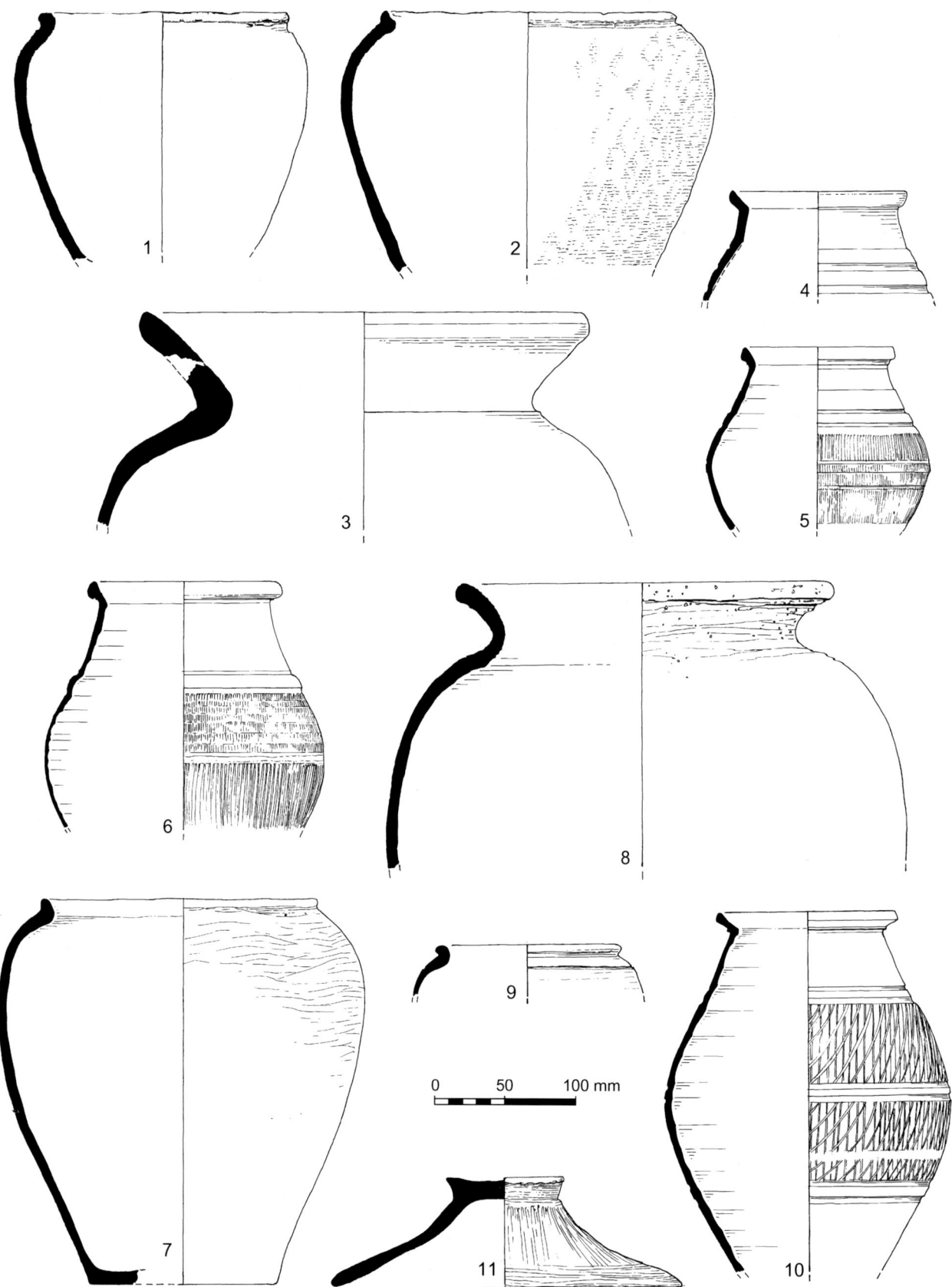

Figure 17 Late Iron Age/Romano-British pottery from Area A South

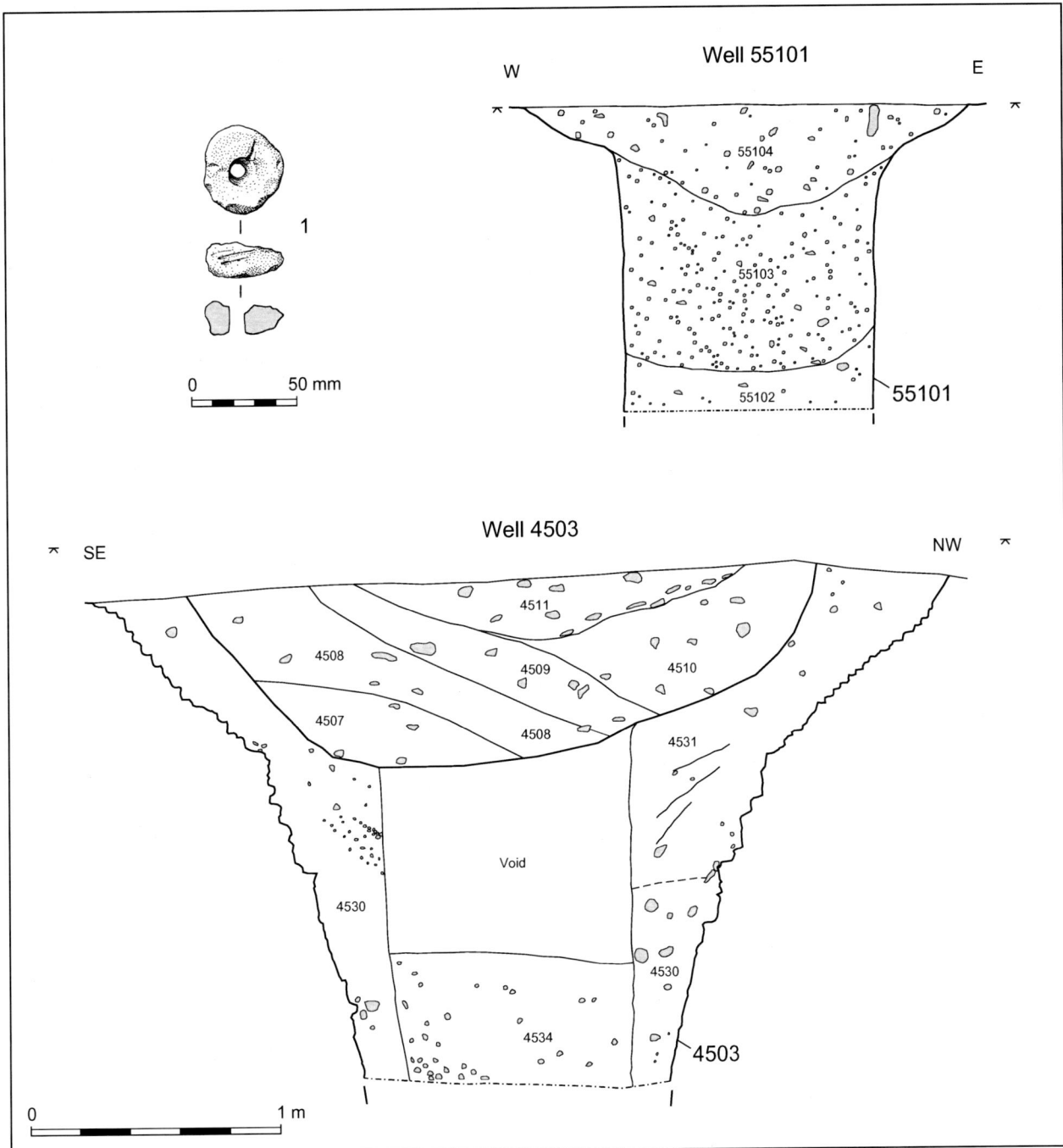

Figure 18 Sections of wells in Area A South and chalk spindlewhorl

Age and Late Iron Age/early Romano-British date. Such structures are often interpreted as granaries and they may have been located north of the ditch to shield them from livestock movements along the trackway and in and out of the southern enclosure (below). The structures were also partly bounded to the west by an undated curving gully (A55644), and possibly gully A55645.

The largest feature north of the trackway was a probable chalk quarry (A55650), measuring 7.0 x 4.0 m and up to 1.7 m deep; its irregular shape and profile suggest a number of separate quarrying episodes. It was subsequently used as a dump for domestic refuse including a complete cattle skull. There were also a number of pits in the area (A55091, A55108, A55124, A55129, A55137, and A55555), varying in size, shape, and profile, but most containing further dumps of domestic waste. The largest of these (A55108), a subrectangular pit measuring 1.6 x 2.2 m and 1.1 m deep with vertical sides and a flat base, had the appearance of a typical storage pit. It was subsequently filled with numerous separate dumps of material, with finds including a copper alloy Nauhiem derivative brooch, probably of late 1st century BC date (Fig. 26, 1), pottery (one sherd re-used as a spindlewhorl), a flint hammerstone, animal bone (including fragments of cattle skull), and charred cereal grain and chaff. Another, smaller pit (A55539), undated but cutting gully 55645, had a very dark upper fill containing animal bone, some of it burnt, and a number of burnt hazelnut shells.

The ditch marking the southern side of the trackway (A55635) ended at the west 8.0 m short of the line of the entrance gap on the north side. For most of its length it was narrower (up to 0.9 m) and shallower (0.3 m) than the ditches to the north, although it expanded to a bulbous, steep-sided terminal 1.5 m wide and 0.65 m deep. It contained animal bone, burnt flint, slag, and pottery.

Immediately west of its terminal was a small rectangular structure (A55154), c. 4.0 x 5.0 m internally, comprising slots along its north and west sides, with post-holes (up to 0.2 m deep) at the four corners and along the east and the south sides. Apart from at the north-east corner and on the east side, all the post-holes had been recut; the recuts all were slightly to the west or south-west of the original cuts. Small quantities of burnt flint and slag were recovered, along with small sherds of Late Iron Age/Romano-British pottery. The slots, which averaged 0.3 m wide, were filled with tightly packed flints. The flints in the northern slot appeared to be concentrated in positions opposite the post-holes on the south side. The alignment of the western slot on the post-hole recuts at the north-west and south-west corners (rather than on the original post-hole cuts) suggests that this slot, at least, dates from the rebuilding of the structure. There were no internal features to the structure, but its function is clearly related to the trackway and the rectangular enclosure to its immediate south (below), possibly providing stockman's accommodation.

South-west of the structure, there was another probable well (A4503). This was sectioned by machine to a depth of 2.0 m revealing a 3.4 m in diameter weathering cone at the top, narrowing with slightly convex sides to 1.2 m at a depth of 1.9 m (Fig. 18). The feature was similar to a well discovered in the 1960s at Oakridge, 1 km to the east and excavated to its full depth of 26 m (Oliver 1992). This had been dug in the late 1st century AD and had gone out of use at end of 2nd century.

The well was immediately north and east of the entrance to a rectangular enclosure, 36 m long and 28–31 m wide, with its long axis and entrance facing north-north-west. Its boundary was defined by a series of ditches (A55638–40), up to 1.2 m wide and 0.3 m deep, indicating that the enclosure had undergone some modification; the slightly outward bowing ditch on its western side, for example, had been replaced by another just outside its original line. The enclosure entrance was marked by a 7.0 m wide gap in the ditch, the terminal on the west side being either cut by, or extended slightly inwards by two small pits. Within the entrance were two post-holes set 3.0 m apart that could indicate a gate or other barrier.

Although most of the dated features inside the enclosure were Early Iron Age and the enclosure appears to bound two of the Early Iron Age roundhouses, the enclosure is clearly related to the other Late Iron Age/early Romano-British features, and small quantities of finds of this period were recovered. Two of the post-holes in Early Iron Age roundhouse A55293 (Fig. 11), for example, contained intrusive Romano-British sherds. Another sherd was recovered from a post-hole (A55322) that formed part of an otherwise undated square five-post structure (A55657). However, these do not amount to convincing evidence that this was a settlement enclosure. Given the occurrence of the square structures (and pits) north of the trackway, it is more likely that it was used as a livestock corral.

Outside the north-west corner of the enclosure, there was a line (c. 5.0 x 2.0 m) of five intercutting subcircular pits (A55037, A55060, and A55079–81), up to 0.7 m deep, with a narrow gully on the same alignment to their north, all of them on the approximate line of the enclosure's western side. They displayed episodes of deliberate backfilling with chalk rubble, interspersed with periods of natural silting, and contained early Romano-British pottery, animal bone, and worked and burnt flint. Fuel ash slag recovered from pit A55079 may be later prehistoric in date and residual. Although of uncertain function, the repeated activity in this one location appears to reflect the spatial organisation of the larger site.

Area A North

Some 100 m north-north-west of the Area A South settlement was a second rectangular enclosure, aligned west-south-west to east-north-east, measuring c. 37 m long by 21 m wide, with a 3.5 m wide, south-facing entrance at its south-west corner (Fig. 19). Its ditch (A55402) had a generally regular V-shaped profile, averaging 1.7 m wide and 0.7 m deep, except at the west where it averaged 1.2 m wide. It appeared to have silted up naturally with no evidence for recutting or maintenance and its use may have been relatively short-lived. There was limited evidence to suggest that its primary fills contained only wares in the native ceramic tradition while the upper fills also contained wheelmade, more Romanised, greywares but this is based on very small context groups, mostly composed of unfeatured sherds. A fragmentary cattle skull was also recovered from the ditch.

There was a number of apparently associated post-holes within the southern half of the enclosure, most of which appeared to be positioned on a grid with the same axes as the enclosure; only one (A55445)

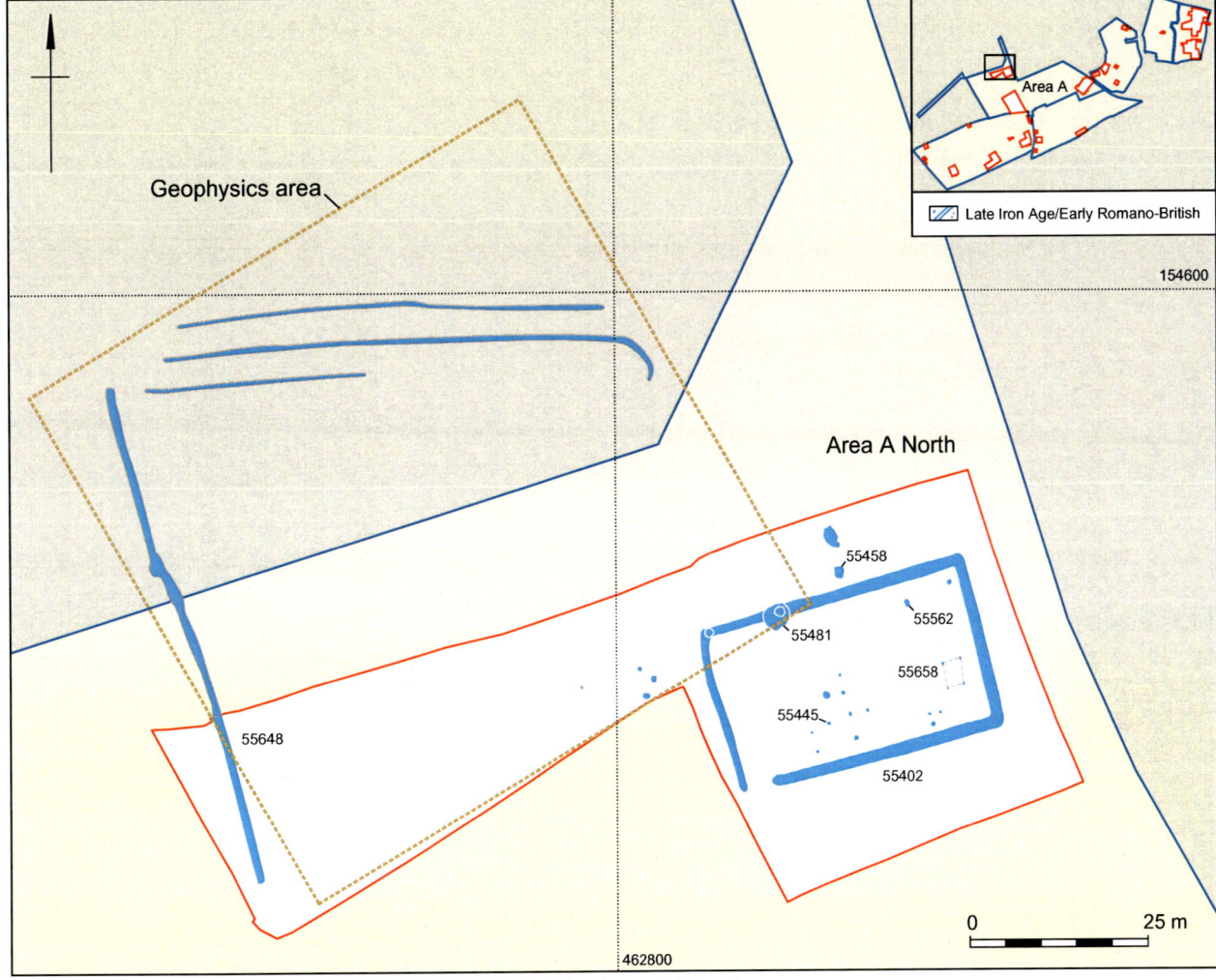

Figure 19 Late Iron Age/Romano-British features in Area A North

produced any dating evidence. Their shallow depths (average 0.12 m) makes it likely that some others had been truncated and, while four at the east end may represent a four-post structure (A55658), its sides (up to 3.5 m long) would make it substantially larger than the square structures in Area A South. The group of eight post-holes to the west, however, did not appear to define a recognisable structure although they could represent the surviving remains of adjacent four-post structures. An alternative interpretation, suggested by the regular spacing and alignment of the post-holes, is that they comprised the surviving elements of a larger rectangular and possibly aisled structure, potentially up to 23 m long and 9.0 m wide. However, these and any other interpretations must remain a matter of speculation.

There were also a number of pits, some inside the enclosure (eg, A55562), some outside (eg, A55458). Others were positioned over, and cutting, the ditch suggesting that some (possibly most) post-dated the use of the enclosure. They varied in size, shape, and profile and, as with those in Area A South, appeared to contain a variety of dumps of domestic waste and other materials. The largest (A55481), a subcircular pit (possibly recut) cutting the enclosure ditch on its north side, was 3.6–4.0 m wide and 1.2 m deep and contained pottery, a rosette brooch of 1st century AD date (Fig. 26, 2), iron nails, worked and burnt flint, and animal bone.

There was an undated ditch (A55648), 67 m west of the northern enclosure, running parallel to its western side; it was shown by geophysical survey to continue for a further 47 m to the north of the excavated area. Its V-shaped profile, up to 1.4 m wide and 0.6 m deep, was comparable to that of the enclosure and the fact that they shared the same orientation as the southern enclosure suggests that they all formed part of the same organised landscape. The geophysical survey also detected three parallel features aligned east–west, also probably ditches spaced *c.* 4 m apart, that may have formed part of the same system of ditches.

Areas D South and North

Although the Romano-British settlement uncovered in Area D comprised many of the same elements as in Area A, including a trackway, enclosures, ditches, structures, and pits, they combined here in a dense complex of intercutting and overlapping features, indicating the repeated reworking, modification, and reorganisation of space over a longer period (Figs 20–22), an inference supported by the mid-1st to the mid–late 4th century AD date range of the pottery (Fig. 25). Although the finely-made bow of a Late Iron Age Nauheim brooch was found in ditch D5295 (below; Fig. 26, 3), the far smaller proportion of pottery fabrics in the native tradition in Area D than in Area A, coupled with the predominance of the wheelmade greywares, suggests that activity started here slightly later although still probably within the third quarter of the 1st century AD.

In addition, the excavation revealed a clear focus of settlement activity, as well as a wider range of settlement structures and facilities, including roundhouses, a waterhole, a corn drier, and other features of less certain function. It is possible that this contrast with Area A relates to the abrupt change in geology between them, the Area D settlement lying on the Reading Beds between the Chalk to the south and the London Clay to the north.

Unfortunately, the different geology reduced the archaeological visibility in Area D, with the result that the stratigraphic relationships between many of the ditches in particular were hard to establish, hampering the identification of separate phases of activity, a problem exacerbated by the chronologically undiagnostic nature of a large proportion of the Romano-British pottery assemblage.

Area D South

The focus of settlement in Area D South (Fig. 21), possibly accessed by a trackway running from the south between two subrectangular enclosures (below), comprised a number of roundhouse gullies, four-post structures, pits, and a waterhole. It was not possible to establish whether the settlement was initially, or at any time, either open or enclosed, although the area appears to have been bounded to the west by a series of intercutting and overlapping ditches and gullies (D5295), some evidently recut. However, at least one (possibly two) of the east-west ditches which lay to the north post-dated one of the roundhouse gullies. This gully (D5303), which was 0.4 m wide and had a projected diameter of some 8.0 m, may have been positioned in the angle of ditch D5294, which appears to turn to the south-west around it. The same ditch, further to the south-west, turned to the south, apparently around the position of

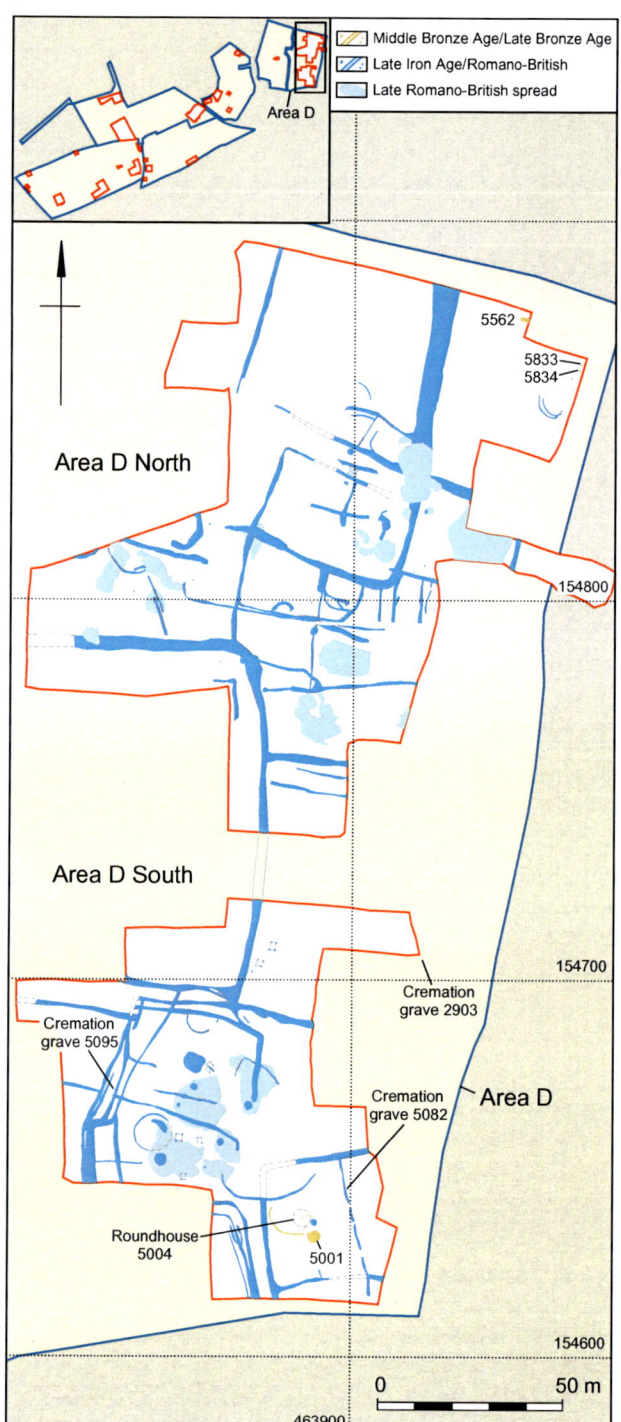

Figure 20 Area D: all phases

a similar roundhouse gully (D5289), suggesting that both structures were already in place when this ditch (and possibly the other ditches) was dug. The southern roundhouse was slightly larger (c. 10 m in diameter), although its south-eastern quadrant, where the entrance is likely to have been positioned, was obscured by a later spread of dark soil (D5027) filling a shallow depression. The only feature within it was a shallow crescent-shaped spread (D5194), c. 5.0 m by 1.6 m, at the north-east, containing pottery and animal bone and possibly indicating an internal activity area. These circular gullies indicate the continued construction of native-style timber roundhouses, although in a slightly different method of construction, during the Romano-British period.

The largest feature within the settlement area was a possible subrectangular waterhole (D5242), measuring 6 x 5 m. A slot was excavated on its northern side which sloped at *c.* 45° to a depth of 0.85 m, with augering suggesting a total depth of 1.6 m. The feature, which appears to have silted up largely naturally, produced Late Iron Age and Romano-British pottery from throughout its excavated fills, including sherds from a long-necked carinated beaker dated to *c.* AD 90–120/130 from the uppermost fill. A short length of truncated gully (D5204) was recorded running towards the feature from the east, surrounded by a cluster of eight post-holes. The post-holes, one of which (D5162) contained clear signs of burning, can be interpreted as two overlapping four-post structures, both *c.* 1.3 m square, one being replaced by another in approximately the same location. To their immediate north was a group of six possible stake-holes, aligned approximately north-south, although any direct association with either the waterhole or the post-holes could not be demonstrated.

A further four four-post structures were recorded in the settlement area – structures D5176 (1.7 m square) and D5300 (1.3 m square) lying east of roundhouse D5289, and structures D5179 (1.6 m square) and D5293 (1.7 m square) towards the north, lying to the east of ditch D5818 which runs north from the settlement area. An arrangement of three unexcavated post-holes (1.5 m apart) south-east of roundhouse D5289, as well as a pair (also 1.5 m apart) south of the waterhole, may also represent the partial remains of similar but truncated structures. The proximity of four-post structure D5176 to roundhouse D5289 (less than 1 m from the projected line of the gully) indicates that these two structures at least were not contemporaneous, but there is little else to indicate the chronological relationship between the four-post structures, either individually or as a group, and other features. The limited dating evidence they contained (which included Romano-British pottery

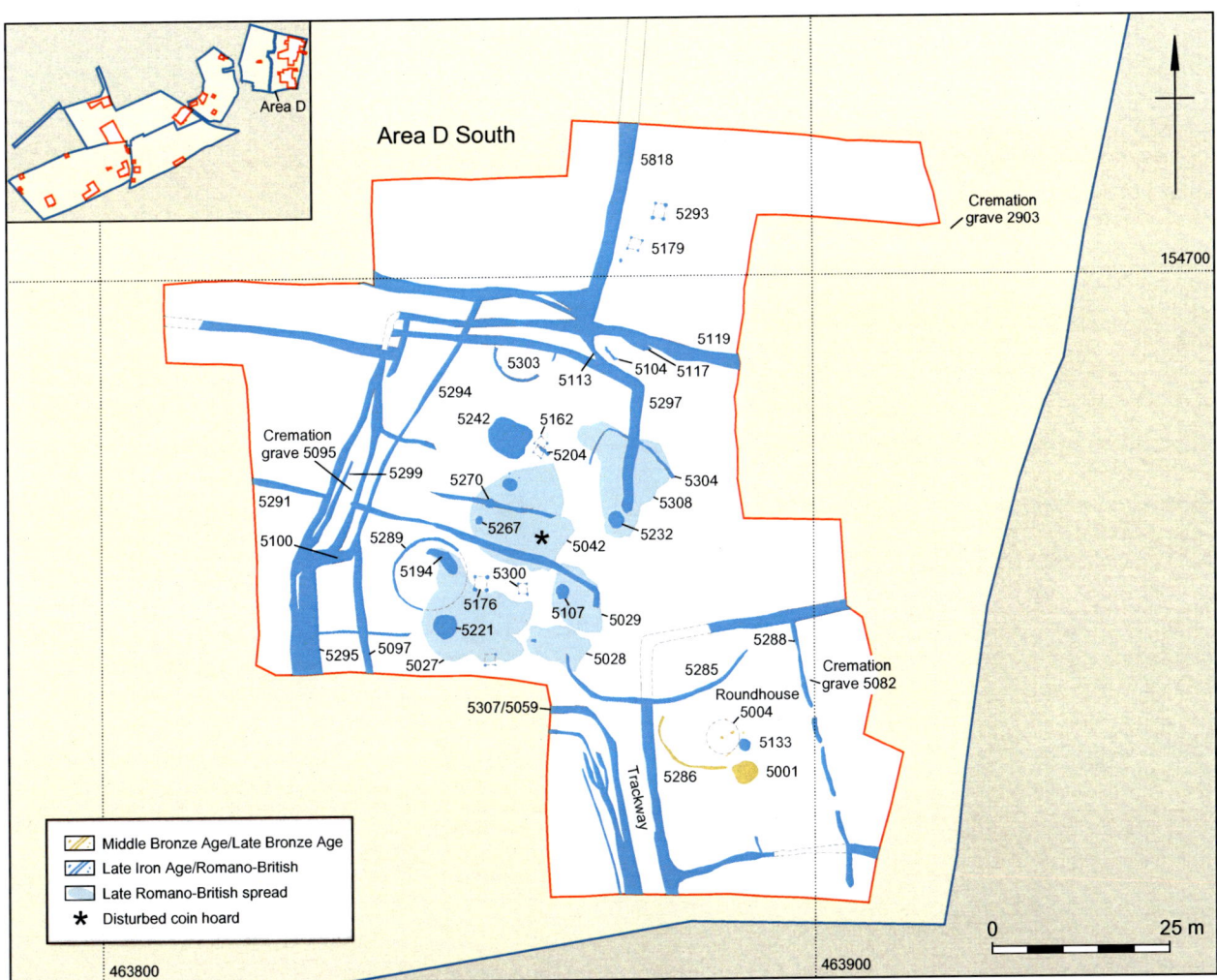

Figure 21 Area D South: all phases

from each of the post-holes in structure D5176) was insufficiently diagnostic to place them within any specific phase of the Romano-British sequence. Nevertheless, they have a clear south-south-west to north-north-east distribution, matching the main orientation of the surrounding ditches to their west.

There were a number of pits within the settlement area (D5107, D5221, D5232, D5267, and D5270), between 1.0 m and 3.0 m in diameter and up to 1.3 m deep, which produced a range of finds consistent with domestic and craft activity, including oyster shell, a worked antler tine, fragments of cattle skull, nails, an iron ring, smithing slag including a hearth bottom, fragments of a Greensand rotary quern and lava querns, and ceramic building material (CBM). Again, most of the pottery was of general Romano-British date, although a number of sherds from pit D5107 were of late 2nd/early 3rd century (mid-Romano-British) date (Fig. 25, 21–2). Other features included a slightly crescent-shaped spread of chalk blocks and flint nodules (D5104), 2.5 m long and 0.4 m wide, containing a number of nails, pottery, oyster shell, and a broken iron knife. Its location, between two of the east–west ditches (D5117 and D5119) at the north of the settlement area, suggests that this possible structure may also have pre-dated these ditches.

Also within this area were a series of quite extensive dark humic deposits (D5027, D5028, D5029, D5042, and D5308) containing quantities of settlement debris, filling shallow hollows that possibly resulted from heavy traffic within the settlement area. Wood charcoal from D5029 included a wide range of species and, therefore, may derive from hedgerows and be indicative of their existence nearby. A number of the settlement features were shown to be sealed by these deposits which may represent the formation of soil following abandonment of the settlement, and a number of 4th century coins recovered from this soil could represent a disturbed hoard. Part of a Nauhiem derivative type brooch (Fig. 26, 4) was recovered from spread D5029.

Ditches ran south, east, north, and west beyond the excavated area indicating that the settlement lay within a more extensively organised and enclosed landscape. These ditches appeared to define a complex of adjacent enclosures or fields, the two enclosures to the south, for example separated by a trackway up to 4 m wide. The only clearly Romano-British feature within the enclosure east of the trackway, which was subdivided by further lengths of ditch, was a pit (D5133), 1.7 m in diameter and 1.0 m deep. It is possible, however, that the adjacent larger pit (D5001), 2.0 m in front of the Middle–Late Bronze Age roundhouse (D5004, above), also belongs to this phase (see above).

A number of ditches also cut across the settlement area. While one unexcavated gully was cut by pit D5270, some of the other ditches are inferred as being later than the settlement, although few stratigraphic relationships were established. Ditch D5291, aligned west-north-west to east-south-east, ran from beyond the western edge of the excavation and, after a short break, crossed over ditch D5294 before passing 1.2 m north of roundhouse D5289; its course then turned south for at least 3.0 m, and in the direction of the trackway. The section excavated north of the roundhouse contained predominantly late Roman pottery, fragments of a perforated fired clay object (probably a loomweight), CBM, fragments of a Greensand rotary quern, and a possible rub-stone. However, its stratigraphic relationships with the humic deposits D5042 and D5029 were not established. Further north, ditch D5297 also crossed over ditch D5294 before turning south for 18 m towards the trackway. Its rounded terminal (adjacent to pit D5232), however, was shown to be sealed by humic deposit D5308. The overall effect of these ditches appears to have been to divide the settlement area into two parts, north and south, each accessible from the northern end of the trackway; their southern extensions possibly designed to aid the movement and control of livestock, while ditch D5119 to their north may have blocked the flow of traffic any further in that direction.

Most of the Romano-British features in Area D South can, therefore, be viewed as components of an evolving arrangement of tracks, settlement, and enclosures. One feature, however, that does not fit easily into this suggested interpretation, was a 25 m long curving gully (D5285), up to 0.7 m wide and 0.6 m deep, lying across the northern end of the trackway and cutting ditch D5286. The pottery from it, which included presumably residual Late Iron Age/early Romano-British sherds, was insufficiently diagnostic to place it within the sequence of Romano-British activity, but its stratigraphic relationship to ditch D5286 suggests that it may have been a late feature, possibly contemporary with, or even post-dating, the extensive dark humic deposits within the settlement area. Another length of L-shaped gully (D5304) which, like gully D5285, does not appear to fit within the wider array of ditches, cut deposit D5308, adding weight to a probable late date for these features, which together appear to form a small D-shaped enclosure.

As described above (see Middle–Late Bronze Age), three unurned cremation burials were recorded within, or just outside, Area D South. While these may have been associated with the prehistoric settlement, it is also possible that they were broadly contemporary with the Romano-British urned cremation graves in Area D North (below).

Area D North

Three Romano-British cremation graves were recorded in Area D North (Fig. 22). All of them lay outside the area bounded by one of the main ditches (D5828) that appears to form two sides of a large subrectangular enclosure or field. Grave D5567, which was 0.9 × 1.1 m, and 0.2 m deep, contained three urned cremation burials aligned north–south (Fig. 23). Burial D5182, of an adult male, was made in a sharply carinated pedestal bowl (ON D8045), dating to *c*. AD 60–150; Fig. 23, 1), while burial D5183, also of an adult, possibly male, was made in a flat-rimmed jar (ON D8044) of a type introduced around AD 90 (Fig. 23, 2), continuing into the middle of the 2nd century. The third burial (D5184), of a person aged 10–14, was made in a south-east Dorset Black Burnished ware jar (ON D8043) whose everted rim suggests a 2nd century date and whose decoration (burnished wavy line around the neck and right-angled lattice decoration) indicates a date in the second half of this century, perhaps several decades later than other two (Fig. 23, 3). Despite the apparent sequence of burials in the one grave only a single backfill was recorded. A few hobnails were found with

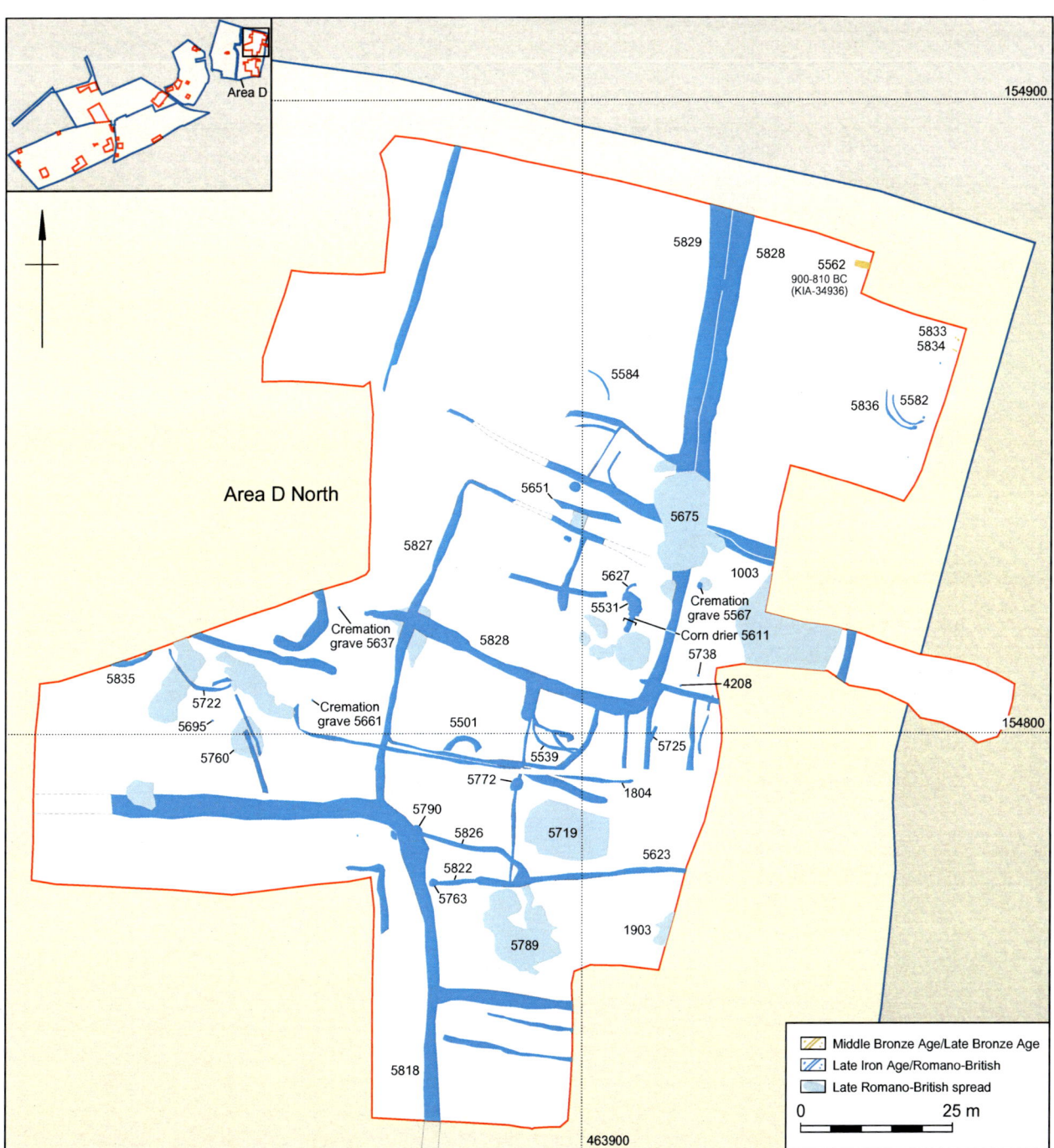

Figure 22 Area D North: all phases

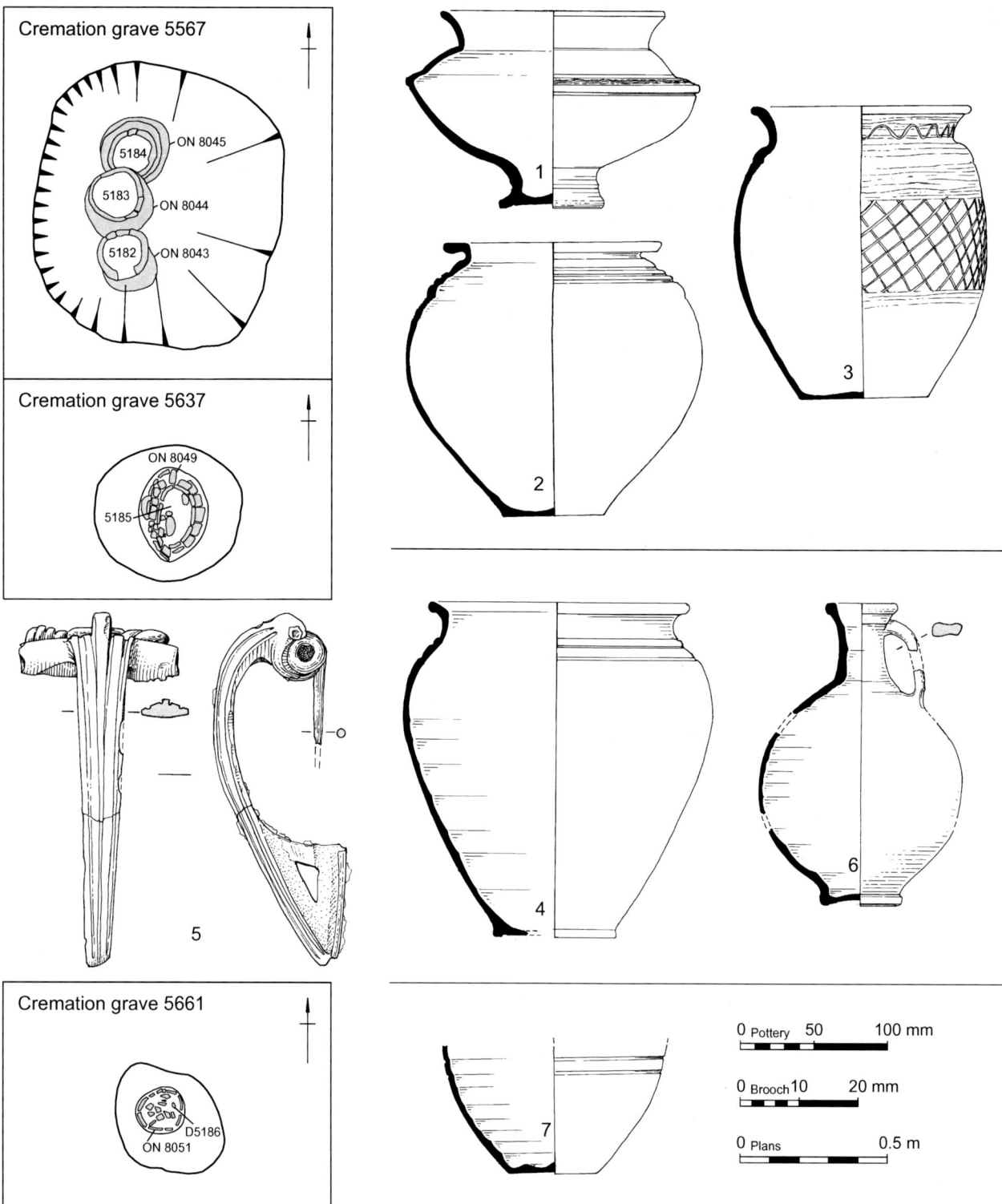

Figure 23 Area D North: cremation graves with selected finds

burial D5183. There were also a few fragments of animal bone (including cattle and bird), and at least two of the cremation deposits contained the remains of chickens that had almost certainly been placed as offerings on the funeral pyre. Although no pyre sites were identified, two small pits (D4208 and D5738) 25 m to the south, contained possible pyre debris including fragments of cremated human bone and charcoal; one also contained a charred tuber of false oat grass, the other fragments of sloe stone.

Two further cremation graves were recorded on the western side of the site (Fig. 22). Grave (D5637), near the western end of ditch D5828, contained an urned cremation burial (D5185; Fig. 23). The urn, a greyware cordoned jar (ON D8049; Fig. 23, 4), contained the remains of an adult female and a brooch dated to the mid-1st century AD (Fig. 23, 5). The grave also contained sherds from a small whiteware flagon (Fig. 23, 6). Approximately 15 m to the south, a similar grave (D5661) contained the base of a greyware jar (ON D8051; Fig. 23, 7, truncated by modern disturbance) and the cremated remains of an adult male (D5186).

Although a number of curved gullies in Area D North, may be the remains of roundhouses, there was no focus of settlement comparable to that to the south, and the presence of the burials may further reflect significant differences in the character of the activities undertaken in this part of Area D. Moreover, none of the gullies was clearly defined and their identification as roundhouses is not certain. Most were situated between enclosure ditch D5828 and ditch D5818, the other main ditch (again bounding a large enclosure) which ran south into Area A South. Gully D5539, formed the south-west arc with a projected diameter of 8.0–9.0 m, while to its west gully D5501, consisted of a north-facing arc with a projected diameter of just 5.0–6.0 m. On the western edge of the site, gully D5722 formed the slightly irregular south-west facing arc of a circle 13 m in diameter, while gully D5835 only just extended into the excavation area, forming part of the southern arc of a circle 10–14 m in diameter. Within the enclosure bounded by ditch D5828, a 6.0 m long curved gully, D5584, formed the north-east arc of a circle with a projected diameter of 10 m; there were no associated features, and no pottery was recovered from it, although fragments of a triangular fired clay loomweight could indicate a date anywhere from the Middle Iron Age through to the Romano-British period.

Near the north-east corner of Area D North, two approximately concentric gullies (D5582 and D5836) formed the south-western arcs of circles with diameters of 7.0–8.0 m (inner gully D5582) and 9.0–10 m (outer gully D5836) respectively. Both were undated, but the use of ring gullies, in contrast to post-rings as found on the Middle Bronze Age and Early Iron Age roundhouses (above), suggests their broad contemporaneity with the Romano-British structures on the site. It is likely, given their relative positions, that the gullies were not contemporaraneous components of a single structure, but represent the rebuilding of a roundhouse at approximately the same location.

The generally non-domestic character of the features in Area D North, is reinforced by the presence of a corn drier (D5611), of which the T-shaped flue and the rounded stoking pit at its southern end survived, with all traces of the drying chamber above having been truncated. The flue's construction cut, oriented north-north-east to south-south-west, was 2.3 m long, 0.9 m wide at the stoking

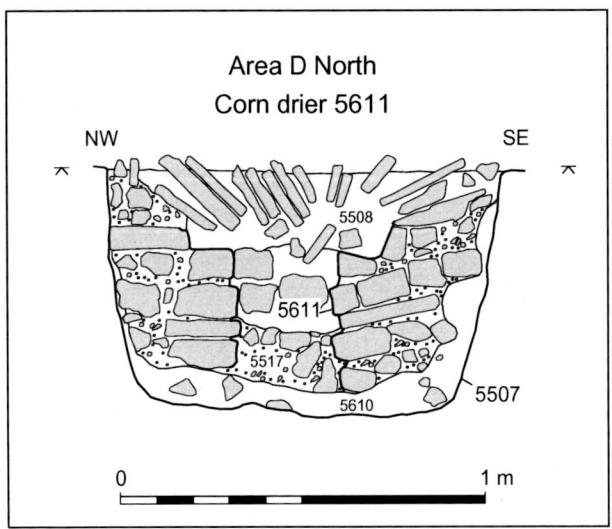

Figure 24 Corn drier in Area D North: section

pit and 1.7 m wide at the cross flue at the back, and 0.6 m deep. The base and sides of the cut were lined with a layer of redeposited clay (up to 0.1 m thick) upon and against which the walls' roughly dressed chalk blocks, bonded with clay, had been constructed. The flue channel was just 0.2 m wide (Fig. 24). At the mouth of the chamber the walls comprised alternating courses of chalk blocks and tile, above which were the collapsed remains of a tile arch. The charcoal-rich fills in the stoke-hole and chamber, contained the charred remains of spelt and hulled wheat and barley. Also found were c. 50 hobnails, a fragment of a rotary quern, lead waste, and animal bone, while the pottery included a sherd of New Forest colour coated indented beaker dated to the 3rd–4th centuries suggesting a late date for the abandonment of the corn drier. Possibly associated with the use of the corn drier was a spread of occupation material (D5531) around its northern end, which contained 4th century pottery and Romano-British brick and tile, which appeared to be flanked by two clusters of stake-holes. To the east these had the same north-north-east to south-south-west orientation as the corn drier and may represent some form of structure such as a lightweight shelter or windbreak. Also possibly associated was a short length of tightly curved gully (D5627) that defined a circular space 3 m in diameter, whose southern end appeared to be sealed by occupation spread D5531. Apart from these features, there was no indication that the corn drier was located within a building, as was the case with a better preserved corn drier found at Manor Farm, Monk Sherborne, c. 3.5 km to the north-west (Teague 2005, fig. 12).

A small number of pits were recorded in Area D North. The precise nature of one small pit (D5695), immediately south of roundhouse gully D5722, is unclear – it contained greyware sherds, some from a

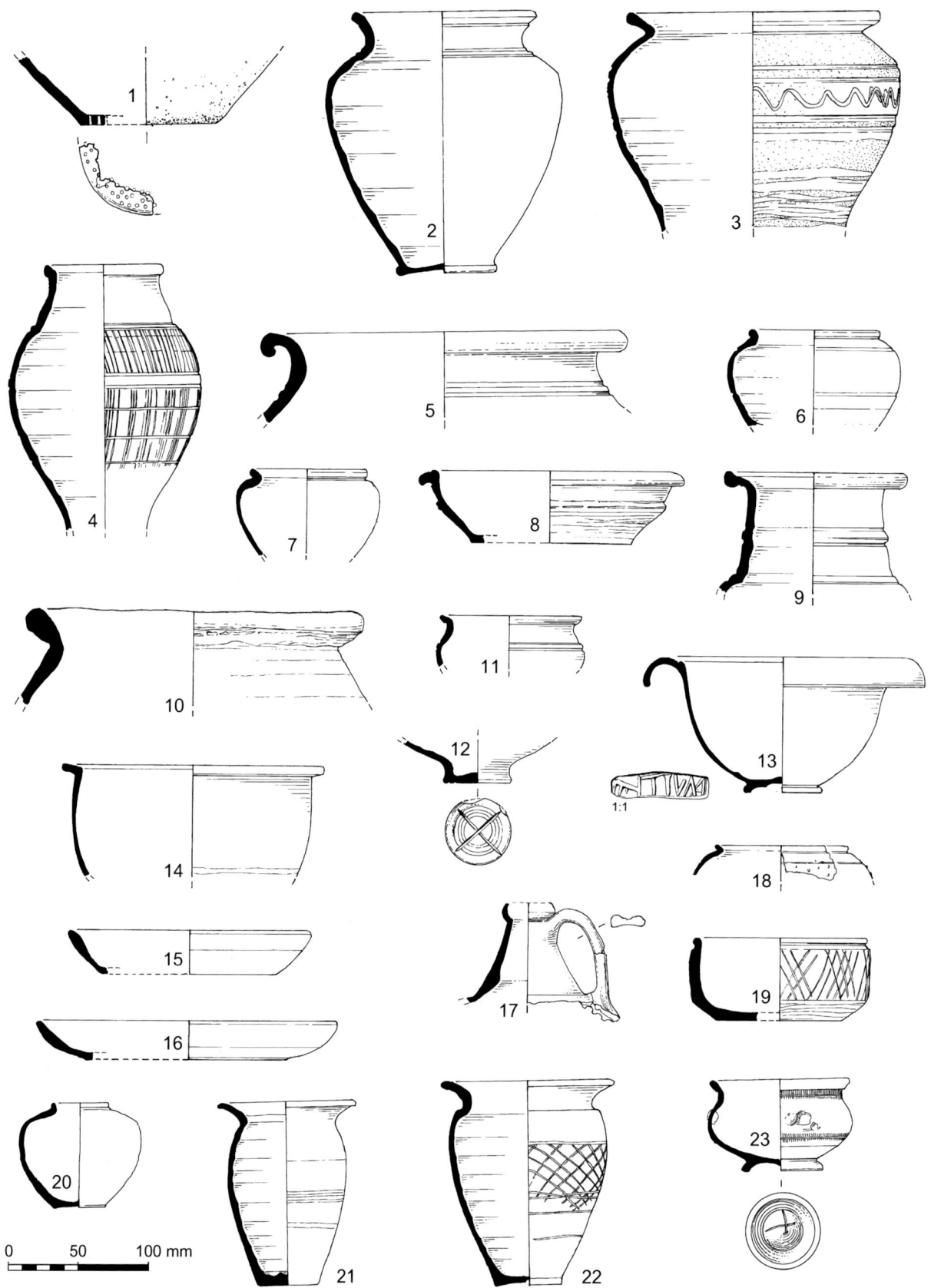

Figure 25 Late Iron Age/Romano-British pottery from Area D

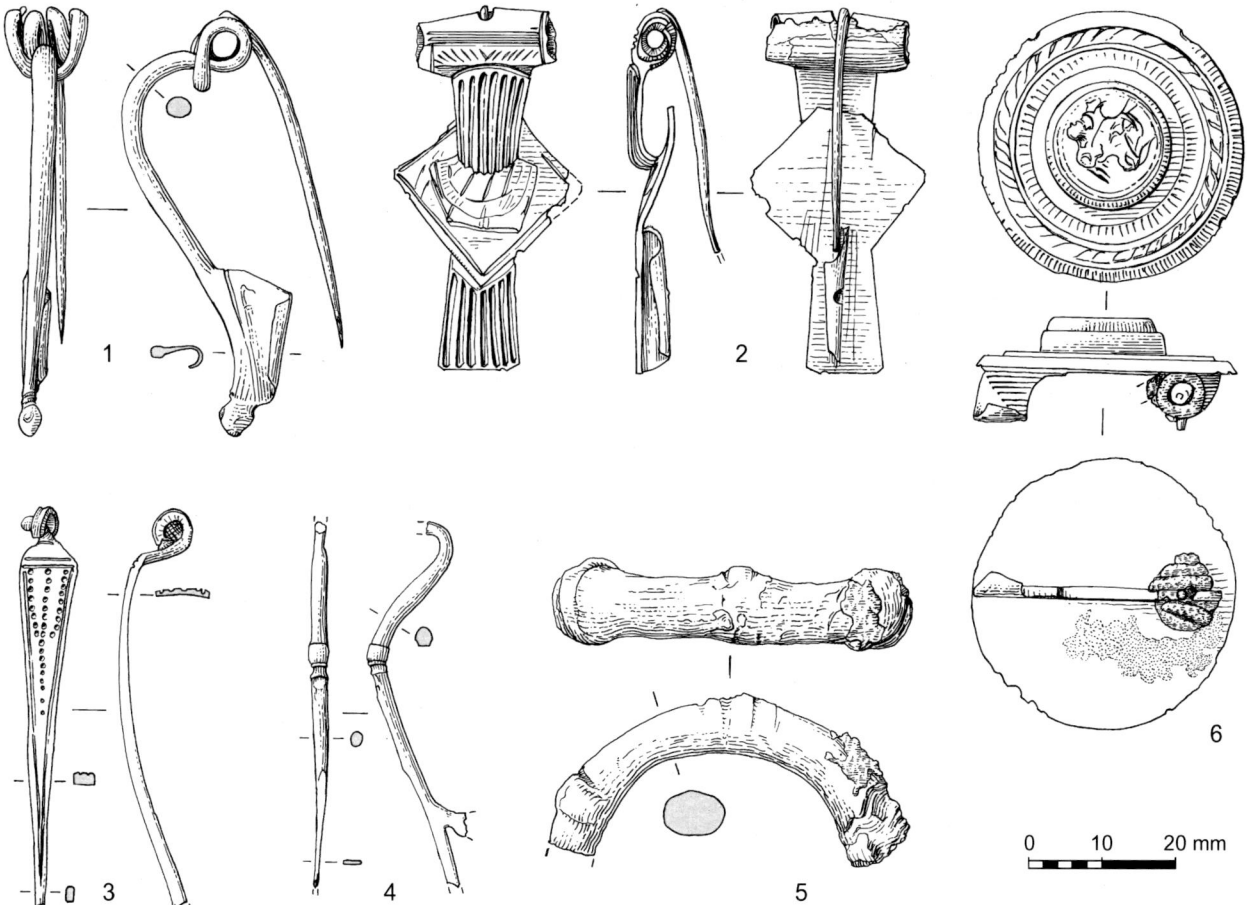

Figure 26 Copper alloy objects

small globular beaker with a beaded rim (Fig. 25, 20), lying on top of Romano-British tiles that had in turn been placed on a large piece of flint, as well as a large quantity of charcoal (and an intrusive fragment of medieval/post-medieval CBM).

Three further pits (D5763, D5772, and D5790), all close together, contained varying quantities of what appeared to be domestic refuse. They all cut a number of interconnected ditches and appeared to have been relatively late features, pit D5772, for example containing a necked bowl of 4th century date (Fig. 25, 23). In addition, partly cutting another ditch, there was an elongated feature (D5725), 3.0 m long, 0.6 m wide and 0.35 m deep, aligned north-north-east to south-south-west, whose shape, with vertical sides and a flat base, suggests some specific function. This was not clear, however, from its dumped, charcoal-rich fill which contained several iron nails and unidentifiable iron objects, CBM, animal bone (some burnt), and pottery, as well as the charred remains of wheat, barley, and weeds. As in Area D South, there were a number of extensive spreads of dark soil that contained occupation debris and 4th century coins. These spreads filled shallow depressions in the underlying natural that may have been caused by heavy traffic by people and animals in these areas and sealed a number of ditches and other features.

As already mentioned, the arrangement of ditches in Area D North was dominated by two main ditches. At the south, ditch D5818, which was up to 3.7 m wide but only 0.5 m deep, was connected to a number of east-west ditches in the north of Area A South. It had a slightly bowed line, running south-north for almost 100 m, before turning to the west to form a relatively large enclosure. However, only a relatively small part of the interior was excavated and only four features were recorded – two short lengths of ditch forming an L-shape, 3.0–5.0 m inside the north-east corner of the enclosure ditch and a small pit and a post-hole. Approximately 26 m m to the north, ditch D5828, which contained sherds of mid-2nd–3rd century date (Fig. 25, 4–19) and part of a terret ring (Fig. 26, 5), was of comparable dimensions and defined a similarly large enclosure, although one on a slightly different orientation. It was cut by a large irregular hollow (D5675), containing mid-2nd–early 3rd century pottery and a late Romano-British disc brooch of 3rd or 4th century date (Fig. 26, 6). As in Area D south, however, the relationship between these ditches and others that ran perpendicular to them was not clearly established, and the changing layout of enclosures and sub-enclosures in this part of the site is unclear. While a range of alternative interpretations are possible, all are conjectural, lacking the stratigraphic and relational data necessary to confirm or disprove them.

Area C

Two large chalk quarries were recorded in Areas C7 and C8 (Fig. 27). The eastern one (C8104), 75 m south-east of the enclosure in Area A South, was sub-oval in plan, c. 12 x 15 m, and 2.2 m deep. Shallow ramps, up to 5.0 m long and 3.0 m wide, ran to its edge from the north-west and the south-east. It had filled up with weathered chalk rubble overlain by layers of predominantly naturally deposited silty clay, although an intervening layer of charcoal-rich material appears to have been a deliberate dump. The western quarry (C9703), which was not fully exposed in plan, appeared to be sub-circular, some 15–19 m wide and 2.3 m deep with a shallow concave profile.

The lowest fill (C9706), which produced early Romano-British pottery, also contained a moderate amount of charcoal. These features are substantially larger than the cluster of intercutting possible quarry pits (A55650) in Area A South (Fig. 16), and there are a number of reasons why chalk might have been extracted on this scale. It may have been used as a building material (either as chalk blocks as found in the Area D corn drier, or for mortar, or as cob where crushed chalk is compacted to form walls, or as daub), or it may have been mixed with clay to create marl for spreading on fields to improve soil fertility; although this would probably not be necessary in areas where the underlying geology was Chalk, it could have been transported to the areas of the Reading Beds and London Clay to the north.

The material from the western pit may have been transported along a nearby trackway, defined by two parallel shallow ruts, c. 1.6 m apart. It was dated by a sherd of Romano-British pottery and a late 3rd century coin recovered from the fill of one of the ruts. The track was traced for 190 m north-west–south-east directly down the slope of the ridge, crossing the

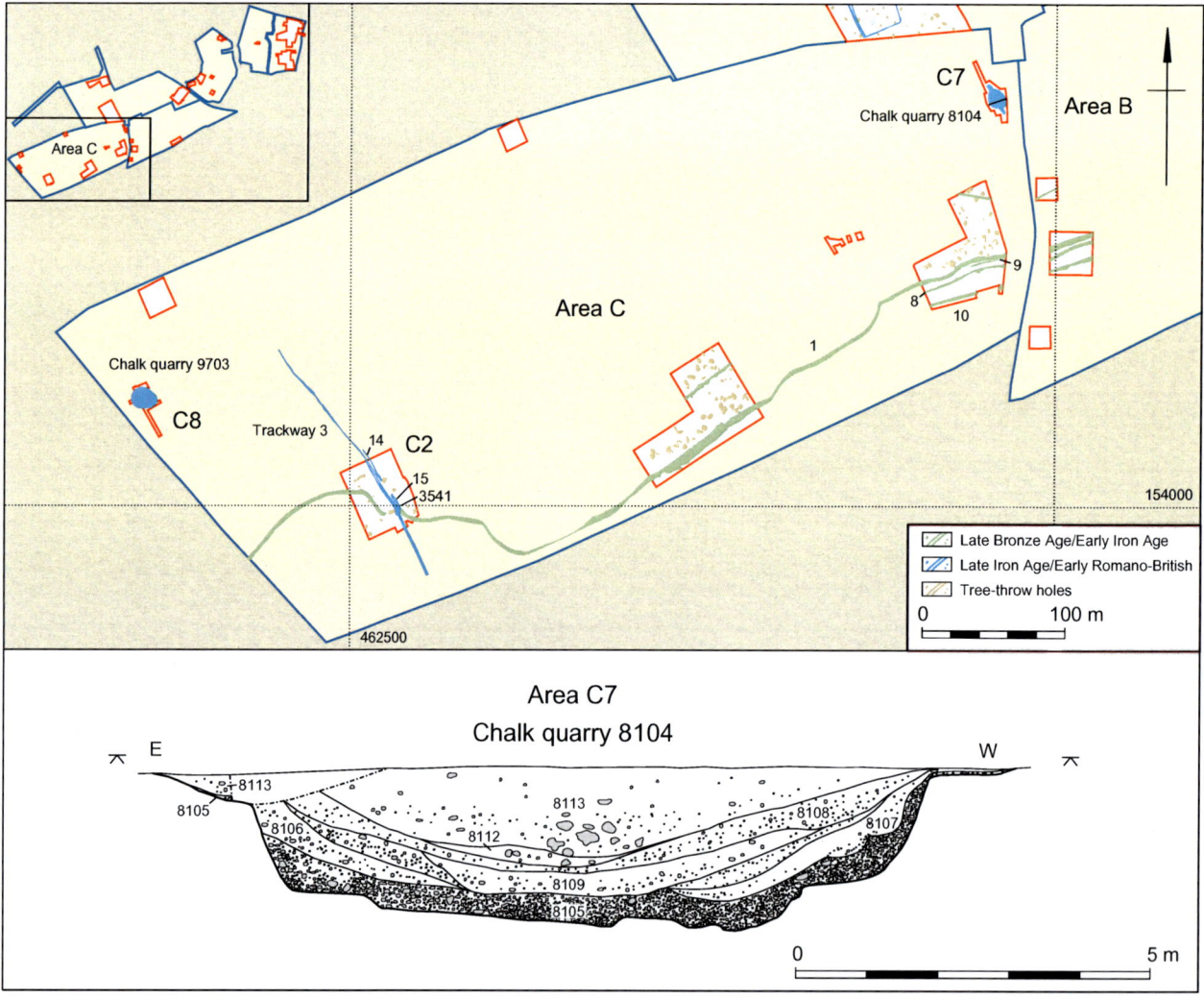

Figure 27 Romano-British features in Area C, with section of quarry C8104

now silted up Wessex Linear ditch where an oval spread of gravel (C3541), 7.0 x 5.0 m and 0.1 m thick, was spread over the ditch fills to provide a more compact surface (Fig. 5). Intermittent linear features (C14 and C15) c. 2.0 m east of, and parallel to the trackway may be additional ruts, possibly created as vehicles negotiated the crossing of the ditch.

Discussion

The Marnel Park and Merton Rise sites lie between two Roman roads running south from Silchester where, following the Conquest, the Atrebatic capital had been retained as the regional administrative centre (*Calleva Atrebatum*). One road ran to Chichester (*Noviomagus*) and the other to Winchester (*Venta Belgarum*), the latter road lying just 1.5 km west of Area A (Fig. 2). The roads would have been constructed soon after the Conquest, and despite the evidence for continuity in material culture, these are likely have had a significant effect on the disposition of settlement within the landscape, and the movement of agricultural and other traded goods across it.

The low levels of potentially Late Iron Age pottery found at Area A suggests that activity there began possibly just before or just after the Conquest, while the absence of samian and Black Burnished ware suggests that it had been abandoned by c. AD 120. The short-lived nature of this and other similar sites points to significant changes in the landscape by the end of the 1st century AD, possibly involving the coalescing of smaller, more dispersed farmsteads into larger agricultural and settlement centres, or the reorganisation of existing farming communities in response to the changing economic climate and the development of new markets for agricultural produce, focused particularly on Silchester.

The Romano-British rectangular enclosures in Area A have numerous parallels in the Basingstoke area, some of which have Late Iron Age predecessors. At Oakridge sites II and IV, immediately south of Popley, an irregular-shaped Late Iron Age/early Romano-British enclosure, that was abandoned by AD 60, was replaced by an arrangement of square and rectangular enclosures or paddocks in the second half of the 1st century (Oliver 1992); further enclosure ditches and possible trackways, revealed in aerial photographs, lie 400 m to the west at Oakridge site VII. Likewise, at Cowdery's Down, c. 3 km east-south-east of Area A, Late Iron Age or early Romano-British activity was succeeded in the mid-1st century AD by a short-lived rectangular enclosure which had reverted to agricultural land by the late Romano-British period (Millett with James 1983). Similar sites have been excavated on the south side of Basingstoke, such as at Danebury Road, Hatch Warren (Brighton Hill South; Howell and Durden 2005), Jays Close, Viables (Millett and Russell 1984; Gibson 2004), and Rucstalls Hill (Oliver and Applin 1978). Such enclosures may have had a specialist function, probably related to animal farming, as suggested by the close association of the southern enclosure in Area A with a possible droveway and by the absence of contemporaneous settlement features within it. The function of the smaller northern enclosure is perhaps less clear although the rectangular arrangement of post-holes might represent some form of stock pens or animal stalls.

In contrast, the complex of features at Area D clearly indicate a continuity of occupation, seen on few of the other sites in the Basingstoke area, that began in the mid-1st century AD and continued up to the mid-late 4th century, the site displaying repeated modification, even the wholesale reorganisation of its layout. It is possible that this contrast relates to the ground conditions on the area of the Reading Beds. Unlike the light, free-draining soils on the Chalk, the clay soils to the north would have been more difficult to work, and more prone to flooding so requiring the repeated recutting of ditches as found in Area D. The poorer quality of the land for both settlement and agriculture may be reflected in the relatively low status of the Marnel Park settlement.

Later Roman activity was also recorded at Oakridge site VII, to the south, where evidence was uncovered of a possible villa dated to the second half of the 4th century, in the form of the remains of a bathhouse with an apsidal end, hypocaust piers, hollow flue tiles, limestone roofing tiles, and painted plaster. Evidence for a possible villa was also found at Monk Sherborne, c. 3.5 km to the north-west, in the form of the remains of a probable winged corridor house, occupied from the mid–late 3rd century (Teague 2005), and a possible aisled building containing a T-shaped corn drier, infilled during the late 4th century. Much of the CBM from the site came from the Area D corn drier, and the small quantities from other contexts are unlikely to be indicative of any substantial, Romanised structure in the immediate vicinity, having perhaps being brought to the site in manure.

In contrast to many of the other Romano-British sites in the area, Area D also provided clear evidence for settlement in the form of roundhouses, as well as including a range of additional features not found in Area A, such as cremation burials, the corn drier, and evidence of smithing. Evidence of iron working and possibly production, consisting of substantial quantities of charcoal, iron slag, and hammerscale, was also recovered from the 3rd century settlement enclosure at Daneshill, c. 2 km to the east which, like the Areas D settlement, was sited on Reading Beds (Millett and Schadla Hall 1991), leading to the suggestion that one of its primary functions was the exploitation of the potential of these deposits for iron ore (*ibid.*, 103).

The presence at Areas A and D of features associated with animal husbandry and structures for the storage of grain points to the mixed agricultural regime practised by the Romano-British population, in a manner possibly little changed from the Iron Age. Analysis of the animal bones showed that cattle and sheep/goat were probably kept in equal numbers supplemented by a fair proportion of pig, a few horses, and dogs. Cattle were kept primarily for dairying and other secondary products, as reflected in a high percentage of mature cattle in the assemblage. As with the pigs, most of the sheep bones, in contrast, had been killed on the brink of adulthood, with excess yearlings killed before they could loose condition during the winter. Beef was probably the main meat eaten, followed by smaller proportions of mutton and pork. The disarticulated nature of the horse remains indicates that they were also eaten. The presence of juvenile domestic fowl indicates poultry keeping, reared for their eggs and feathers, but also used in religious practices as indicated by finds from the cremation graves; wild species, however, were not important in the diet.

The animal husbandry strategies would have complemented the arable farming, with sheep grazing on the stubble after the harvest and manuring the field at the same time, and cattle being used to pull the plough. It is likely that spelt wheat and barley were cultivated on the lighter soils rather than the heavier clay, the flint nodules in the upper fill of the Wessex Linear ditch, for example possibly resulting from a change of landuse from pastoral to arable on the Chalk; pulses were also grown. The final stages of crop processing were undertaken within the settlement, and while the presence of a corn drier (in Area D) and four post-structures raises the possibility of cereal processing and storage on some scale, this might not have been more than the domestic requirements for one or two extended families.

No evidence was recovered among the plant remains from the settlements for the fruits or condiments often associated with more urban or higher status sites at this time, and there were few oyster shells. Despite the possible proximity of villa settlements in the landscape, there were also few artefacts to indicate significant wealth. A few fragments of blue/green vessel glass indicate limited access to the more exotic materials. Only one piece, from the dark earth, could be more closely identified as the base of a square bottle, with a flower design in relief on its base, dated to the mid-1st–late 2nd centuries AD. The overall impression of the Romano-British occupation was of a distinctly rural, agricultural settlement, largely self-sufficient and, although partly Romanised, continuing a pattern of settlement and farming firming rooted in its native, Iron Age predecessors.

Bibliography

Barclay, A., 1999. Grooved Ware from the Upper Thames region, in R. Cleal and A. MacSween (eds), *Grooved Ware in Britain and Ireland*, Oxford: Neolithic Stud. Grp Seminar Pap. 3, 177–206

Barclay, A., 2002. Ceramic lives, in A. Woodward and J.D. Hill (eds), *Prehistoric Britain: the ceramic basis*, Oxford: Prehist. Ceram. Res. Grp Occas. Public. 3, 85–95

Barclay, A., 2004. Earlier prehistoric pottery, in A. Brossler, R. Early and C. Allen, *Green Park (Reading Business Park). Phase 2 Excavations 1995 - Neolithic and Bronze Age Sites*, Oxford: Thames Valley Landscapes Monogr. 19, 57–8

Barfield, L.H., 1991. Hot stones: hot food or hot baths?, in I. Hodder and L.H. Barfield (eds), *Burnt Mounds and Hot Stone Technology: papers from the second international Burnt Mound Conference 1990*, Sandwell: Metropol. Borough Counc.

Boismier, W.A., Mepham, L. and Allen, M.J., 1988. Later prehistoric features at land off Chineham Lane, Sherborne St. John, Basingstoke, Hampshire, *Proc. Hampshire Fld Club Archaeol. Soc.* 53, 25–33

Bowen, H.C., 1978. 'Celtic' fields and 'ranch' boundaries in Wessex, in S. Limbrey and J. Evans (eds), *The Effect of Man on the Landscape: the lowland zone*, London: Counc. Brit. Archaeol. Res. Rep. 21, 115–23

Brown, L., 2000. The regional ceramic sequence, in B. Cunliffe, *The Danebury Environs Programme: The Prehistory of a Wessex Landscape. Volume 1, Introduction*, Oxford: English Heritage/Oxford Univ. Comm. Archaeol. Monog. 48, 79–127

Bradley, P., 1999. Worked flint, in A Barclay and C Halpin, *Excavations at Barrow Hills, Radley, Oxfordshire. Volume 1: the Neolithic and Bronze Age monument complex*, Oxford: Thames Valley Landscapes Monogr. 11, 211–24

Bradley, R., Entwistle, R. and Raymond, F., 1994. *Prehistoric Land Divisions on Salisbury Plain: the work of the Wessex Ditches Project*, London: Engl. Herit. Archaeol. Rep. 2

Burgess, C., 1980. *The Age of Stonehenge*, London: Dent

Butterworth, C.A., 1994. Rooksdown Hospital, Basingstoke, Hampshire, in A.P. Fitzpatrick and E.L. Morris (eds) *The Iron Age in Wessex: recent work*, Salisbury: Wessex Archaeol. 76–8

CgMS, 1997. *An Archaeological Desk Based Assessment of Popley Fields, Basingstoke, Hampshire*, unpubl. rep.

CgMS, 2002. *An Archaeological Desk Based Assessment of North Popley, Basingstoke, Hampshire*, unpubl. rep.

Clarke, D.L., 1970. *Beaker Pottery of Great Britain and Ireland*, Cambridge: Univ. Press

Cleal, R.M.J., 1991–3. Pottery, in F. Healy, The excavation of a ring ditch at Englefield by John Wymer and Paul Ashbee, 1963, *Berkshire Archaeol. J.* 74, 18–21

Coe, D. and Newman, R., 1992. Area U, Brighton Hill South, Basingstoke Hampshire: archaeological watching brief and excavation, *Proc. Hampshire Fld Club Archaeol. Soc.* 48, 5–21

Cotton, J., 2004. Surrey's early past: a survey of recent work, in J. Cotton, G. Crocker and A. Graham (eds), *Aspects of Archaeology and History in Surrey: towards a research framework for the county*, Guildford: Surrey Archaeol. Soc. 19–38

Cunliffe, B., 1991. *Iron Age Communities in Britain* (3rd edn), London: Routledge

Fasham, P.J., 1985. *A Prehistoric Settlement at Winnall Down, Hampshire*, Winchester: M3 Archaeol. Rescue Comm. Rep. 8

Fasham, P.J., Keevill G. with Coe, D., 1995. *Brighton Hill South (Hatch Warren): an Iron Age farmstead and deserted medieval village in Hampshire*, Salisbury: Wessex Archaeol. Rep. 7

Fasham, P.J., Farwell, D.E. and Whinney, R.J.B., 1989. *The Archaeological Site at Easton Lane, Winchester*, Winchester: Hampshire Fld Club Archaeol. Soc. Monogr. 6

Gardiner, J., 1988. *The Composition and Distribution of Neolithic Surface Flint Assemblages in Central Southern England*, unpubl PhD thesis, Univ. Reading

Garrow, D., 2007. Placing pits: landscape occupation and depositional practice during the Neolithic in East Anglia, *Proc. Prehist. Soc.* 73, 1–24

Gibson, C., 2004. The Iron Age and Roman site of Viables Two (Jays Close), Basingstoke, *Hampshire Stud.* 59, 1–30

Hawkes, J.W., 1985. The pottery, in P. Fasham, *The Prehistoric Settlement at Winnall Down, Winchester: excavation of MARC3 Site R17 in 1976 and 1977*, Winchester: Hampshire Fld Club Archaeol. Soc. Monogr. 2, 69–76

Healy, F., 1985. The struck flint, in S. J. Shennan, F. Healy and I. F. Smith, The excavation of a ring ditch at Tye Field, Lawford, Essex, *Archaeol. J.* 142, 177–207

Howell, L. and Durden, T., 2005. Further excavation of an Iron Age enclosure at Danebury Road, Hatch Warren, Basingstoke, Hampshire, 1995, *Hampshire Stud.* 60, 39–63

Lewis, E.R. and Walker, G., 1977. A Middle Bronze Age site at Westbury, West Meon, Hampshire, *Proc. Prehist. Soc.* 33, 33–45

Longworth, I., 1971. The Neolithic pottery, in G.J. Wainwright and I.H. Longworth, *Durrington Walls: Excavations 1966–1968*, London: Rep. Res. Comm. Soc. Antiq. London 29, 48–155

Longworth, I. and Cleal R.M.J., 1999. Grooved Ware gazetteer, in R. Cleal and A. MacSween (eds), Oxford: Neolithic Stud. Grp Seminar Pap. 3, 177–206

McOmish, D., Field, D. and Brown., G., 2002. *The Field Archaeology of the Salisbury Plain Training Area*, Swindon: English Heritage

Millett, M. with James, S., 1983. Excavations at Cowdery's Down, Basingstoke, Hampshire, 1978-81. *Archaeol. J.* 140, 151–279

Millett, M. and Russell, D., 1984. An Iron Age and Romano-British site at Viables Farm, Basingstoke, *Proc. Hampshire Fld Club Archaeol. Soc.* 40, 49–60

Millett, M. and Schadla-Hall, T., 1991. Rescue excavations on a Bronze Age and Romano-British site at Daneshill, Basingstoke, 1980–81, *Proc. Hampshire Fld Club Archaeol. Soc.* 47, 83–105

Moffett, L., Robinson, M.A. and Straker, S., 1989. Cereals, fruit and nuts: charred plant remains from Neolithic sites in England and Wales and the Neolithic economy, in A. Milles, D. Williams and N. Gardner (eds), *The Beginnings of Agriculture*, Oxford: Brit. Archaeol. Rep. S496, 243–61

Morris, E.L., 1992. The pottery, 13–23 in D. Coe and R. Newman, Area U, Brighton Hill South, Basingstoke, Hampshire: archaeological watching brief and excavation, *Proc. Hampshire Fld Club Archaeol. Soc.* 48, 5–26

Needham, S., 2005. Transforming Beaker culture in north-west Europe; processes of fusion and fission, *Proc. Prehist. Soc.* 71, 171–217

Oliver, M., 1992. Excavation of an Iron Age and Romano-British settlement site at Oakridge, Basingstoke, Hampshire, 1965–6, *Proc. Hampshire Field Club Archaeol Soc.* 48, 55–94

Oliver, M. and Applin, B., 1978. Excavation of an Iron Age and Romano-British settlement at Ruckstalls Hill, Basingstoke, Hampshire, 1972–5, *Proc. Hampshire Fld Club Archaeol. Soc.* 35, 41–92

Perry, B.T., 1970. Iron Age enclosures and settlements on the Hampshire chalklands, *Archaeol. J.* 86, 29–43

Robinson, M., 2000. Further considerations of Neolithic charred cereals, fruit and nuts, in A. Fairbairn (ed.), *Plants in Neolithic Britain and Beyond*, Oxford: Neolithic Stud. Grp Seminar Pap. 5, 85–90

Smith, K., 1977. The excavation of Winklebury Camp, Basingstoke, Hampshire, *Proc. Prehist. Soc.* 43, 31–129

Teague, S., 2005. Manor Farm, Monk Sherborne, Hampshire: Archaeological investigation in 1996, *Proc. Hampshire Fld Club Archaeol. Soc.* 60, 64–135

Thompson, A., 1983. The pottery, in Millett with James 1983, 182–7